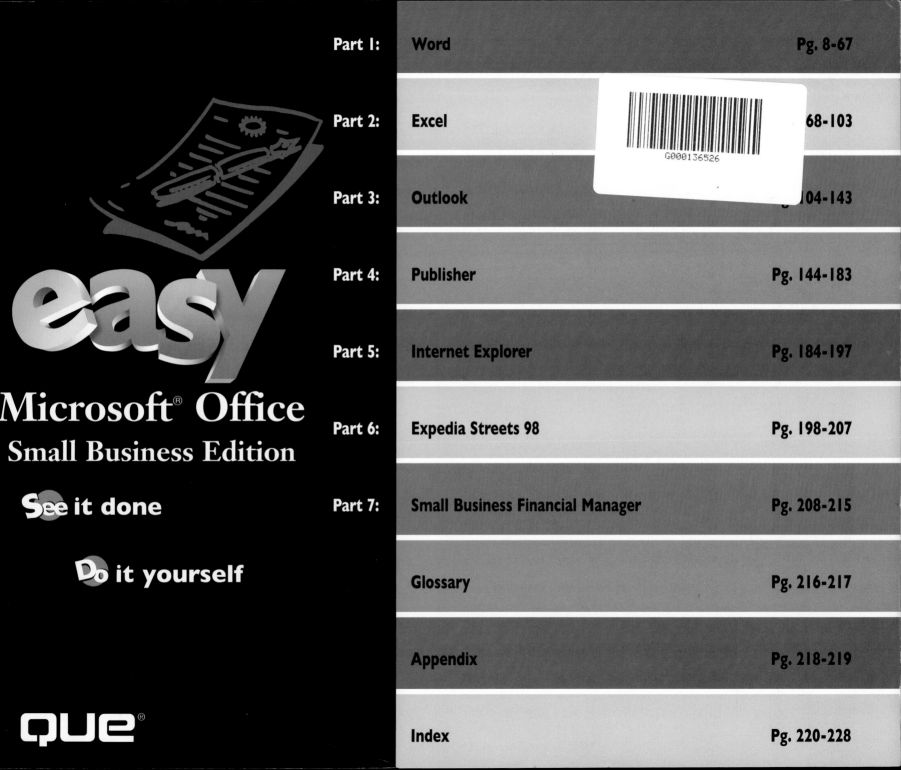

easy

Microsoft® Office
Small Business Edition

See it done

Do it yourself

que®

G000136526

Part ▶ 3: Outlook

Part ▶ 4: Publisher

Copyright© 1998 by Que® Publishing

Library of Congress Catalog No.: 98-84200

ISBN: 0-7897-1638-0

99 98   6 5 4 3 2 1

Interpretation of the printing code: the rightmost double-digit number is the year of the book's printing; the rightmost single-digit number, the number of the book's printing. For example, a printing code of 98-1 shows that the first printing of the book occurred in 1998.

Screen reproductions in this book were created using Collage Plus from Inner Media, Inc., Hollis, NH.

Executive Editor
Karen Reinisch

Acquisitions Editor
Jamie Milazzo

Development Editor
Renee Wilmeth

Managing Editor
Thomas F. Hayes

Project Editor
Lori A. Lyons

Copy Editor
Linda Seifert

Indexer
Tim Wright

Book Designer
Jean Bisesi

Cover Designer
Anne Jones

Production Designer
Trina Wurst

Proofreader
Svetlana Dominguez

How to Use this Book

It's as Easy as 1-2-3

Each part of this book is made up of a series of short, instructional lessons, designed to help you understand basic information that you need to get the most out of your computer hardware and software.

Click: Click the left mouse button once.

Double-click: Click the left mouse button twice in rapid succession.

Right-click: Click the right mouse button once.

Pointer Arrow: Highlights an item on the screen you need to point to or focus on in the step or task.

Selection: Highlights the area onscreen discussed in the step or task.

Click & Type: Click once where indicated and begin typing to enter your text or data.

 Tips and Warnings give you a heads-up for any extra information you may need while working through the task.

2 Each task includes a series of quick, easy steps designed to guide you through the procedure.

Drag

Drop

How to Drag: Point to the starting place or object. Hold down the mouse button (right or left per instructions), move the mouse to the new location, then release the button.

1 Each step is fully illustrated to show you how it looks onscreen.

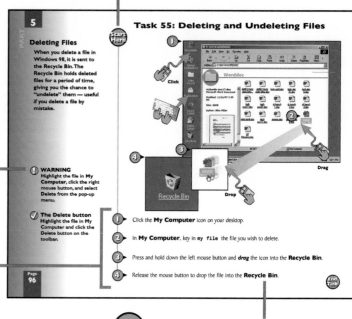

3 Items that you select or click in menus, dialog boxes, tabs, and windows are shown in **bold**.

 Next Step: If you see this symbol, it means the task you're working on continues on the next page.

 End Task: Task is complete.

Introduction

Easy Microsoft Office Small Business Edition is just what its name implies—an easy way to get started with the software that makes up Office SBE. It's easy because it's a step-by-step illustrated guide to using the tools you find in this software package.

If you're like most computer users today, you want to know the easiest way to get up and running fast, particularly when it comes to learning new software. You don't have time to sit down and labor through a book the size of a small suitcase that covers every bell and whistle available in a program. You just need to know the quickest way to accomplish your daily computing tasks. Right? If any of this sounds like you, then you're holding the right book for the job.

This book presents the easiest, most visual way to learn all the basic tools found in each Office SBE program, without rehashing all the fundamental skills you already have. In other words, I'm assuming you already know how to operate in the Windows environment—use the mouse, work with menus and dialog boxes, open and close software, and so on. Rather than explaining what you already know, this book jumps right in and starts exploring each important feature, task by task. You can see clearly what each feature or command can do. Skip around to the topics you want to learn, or review features you may already be familiar with.

In no time at all, you'll have mastered the entire suite of programs and can apply them to your own small business needs. When it comes to computer software these days, if it's not easy, why bother?

PART 1

Word

Microsoft Word is one of the most popular, best-selling word processing programs ever created. You can use Word to create all manner of documents, such as letters, memos, reports, manuscripts, newsletters, and more. When it comes to working with text, there's no match for Microsoft Word.

In this part of the book, you learn all the basic features and skills required to use Word 97. This includes everything from formatting and manipulating text to perfecting your documents with Word's spelling and grammar tools.

As part of the Office Small Business Edition suite of programs, you can put Word's many features to work for you and your small business needs. For example, you can quickly produce business correspondence, fax covers, employee manuals, and more. Whenever you need to create a document, Word is the program to use; as soon as you open the program, a blank document file is waiting for you to start entering text. The toolbars at the top of the program window give you quick access to the most commonly used commands. After you complete a document, save it, print it, and move on.

Tasks

Task 1: Entering Text

Automatic Word Wrap

To enter text into a Word document, just start typing. When you reach the right margin, keep typing. Word automatically wraps the text to the next line for you. Use the **Enter** key only to start a new paragraph.

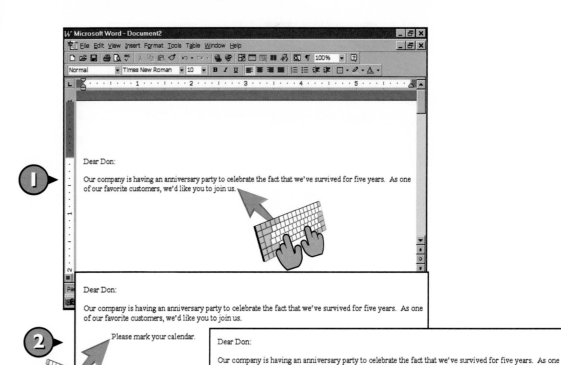

✓ Quick Fix

Press the **Backspace** key to delete the previous character if you make a mistake. You can also use the **Backspace** key to fix things if you accidentally press the **Enter** key or the **Tab** key.

1 Enter the characters and let Word wrap the text when you get to the right margin. Press the **Enter** key to start a new paragraph.

2 Press the **Tab** key to indent the first line of a paragraph.

3 Press the **Caps Lock** key to type all capital letters.

Task 2: Selecting Text with the Mouse

Start Here

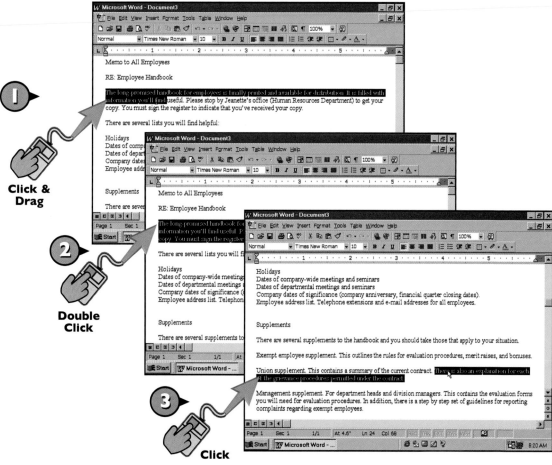

Click & Drag

Double Click

Click

Selecting Text

There are all sorts of things you can do to change the way your text looks, or to move it from one place to another; but before you can do any of these things you must first select (highlight) the text. Word offers lots of ways to select text with your mouse, and these are the most common.

 Unselecting
To unselect text you've already selected, simply click or press any arrow key.

 Quick Select
A triple-click of the mouse button will select the entire sentence.

Place your mouse pointer at the beginning of the text you want to select, then click and drag the pointer until all the text is highlighted.

Select a paragraph by positioning your mouse to the left of the paragraph until the pointer is facing northeast; then double-click.

Select a sentence by holding down the **Ctrl** key and then click anywhere in the sentence.

End Task

Task 3: Selecting Text with the Keyboard

Selecting Text

If you're more comfortable with the keyboard than the mouse, you can select text quickly with key combinations. Move your cursor to the text you want to select and try any of these combinations to select text.

Start Here

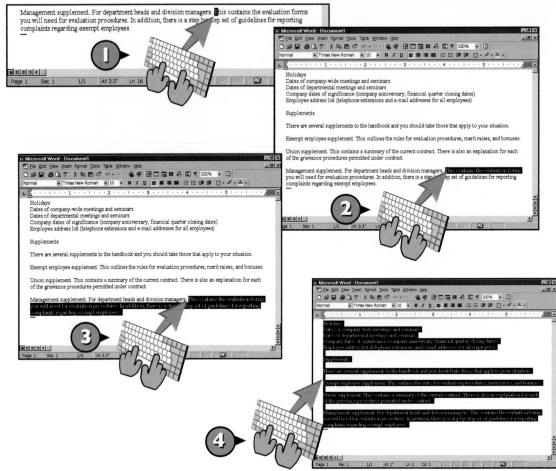

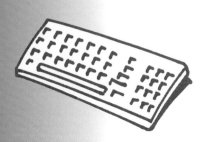

✓ **Deselecting**
To get rid of the highlighting (deselect the text), press any arrow key.

1 Select the character to the right of your cursor by pressing **Shift+Right Arrow**. Keep pressing the **Right Arrow** to include the next character(s).

2 Select everything from your cursor to the end of the line by pressing **Shift+End**. (Use **Shift+Home** to select everything to the beginning of the line.)

3 Select everything from your cursor to the end of a paragraph by pressing **Ctrl+Shift+Down Arrow**. (Use **Ctrl+Shift+Up Arrow** to select everything to the top of the paragraph.)

4 Press **Ctrl+A** to select all the text in the document.

End Task

Task 4: Moving Text

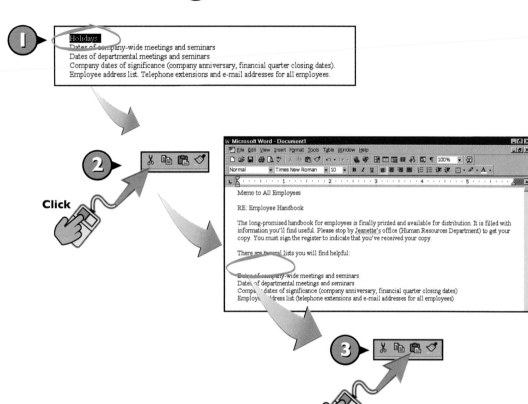

Click

Click

Using the Cut and Paste Commands

You can move text from one place in your document to another. The jargon for this action is *cut and paste.*

1. Select the text you want to move.

2. Click the **Cut** button on the toolbar. The text disappears from your document.

3. Move to the location where you want the text to appear, click to position the cursor, and then click the **Paste** button on the toolbar. The text appears in the new location.

✔ **Cut Shortcut**
The keyboard shortcut for cutting text after you select it is **Ctrl+X.**

✔ **Paste Shortcut**
The keyboard shortcut for pasting text in a new location is **Ctrl+V.**

✔ **Quick Delete**
Use the **Cut** command to quickly delete selected text.

Task 5: Copying Text

Using the Copy and Paste Commands

Copying text is useful when you have to use the same text in several locations. The copied text can include any characters, so you could use this feature for a line of asterisks or any other special characters.

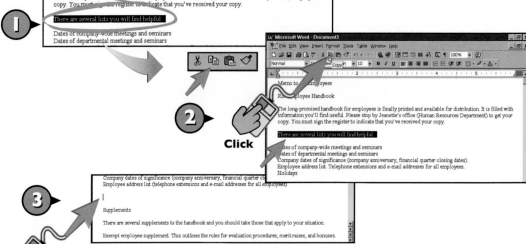

Click

Click

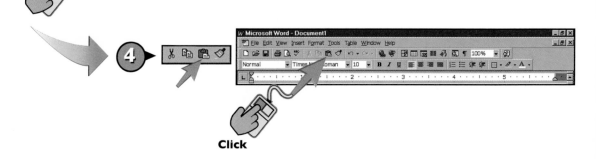

Click

Click

✓ **Copy Shortcut**
The keyboard shortcut for Copy is **Ctrl+C**.

✓ **Multiple Copies**
You can keep pasting multiple copies of the same copied data as many times as you need; just keep clicking the **Paste** button for each new location.

1 ▶ Select the text you want to copy.

2 ▶ Click the **Copy** button on the toolbar. The selected text remains in its place in your document.

3 ▶ Move to the position where you want another copy of the text to appear, and click to position the cursor.

4 ▶ Click the **Paste** button on the toolbar. The text appears in the new location.

Task 6: Changing the Font and Size of Text

Click

Click

Working with Fonts and Sizes

You can change the font or size (or both) of any text in your document. A font is a collection of characters that share the same look, and Word offers lots of fonts to choose from. Font size, of course, is the size of your text. Font size is measured in points; a point is 1/72nd of an inch.

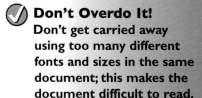

✓ **Don't Overdo It!**
Don't get carried away using too many different fonts and sizes in the same document; this makes the document difficult to read.

✓ **It's Alphabetized!**
Because the Font drop-down list is alphabetized, you can quickly locate the font you're looking for by typing its first letter. This scrolls the list to that particular alphabetized section.

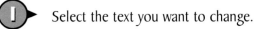

1 Select the text you want to change.

2 Click the **Font drop-down arrow** to display a list of available fonts. Scroll through the list and click the font name you want to use. The font is applied to your text.

3 Click the **Font Size drop-down arrow** to display a list of available sizes. Scroll through the list and click a new size. The size is applied to selected text.

Task 7: Changing the Alignment of Text

Working with Alignment Options

When you enter text, it is automatically aligned with the left margin unless you change the alignment. Alignment controls the horizontal placement of text in your document. You can change the alignment to right, center, or justified.

✓ **Alignment Tip**
Use right-aligned text for columns of numbers to make the numbers line up.

✓ **Justify Paragraphs**
Justifying text won't work unless you have enough words to space across the width of your document. Justified text is commonly used with columns and newsletters.

✓ **Default Alignment**
If you change the text alignment and decide you prefer the default left alignment, select the text and click the **Align Left** button on the toolbar.

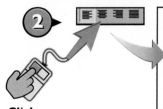

Click

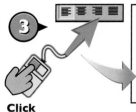

Click

Click

1 Select the text you want to change.

2 To center text, click the **Center** button on the toolbar.

3 To align text against the right margin, click the **Align Right** button on the toolbar.

4 To have your text stretch across the page from margin to margin, click the **Justify** button on the toolbar.

Task 8: Changing the Formatting of Characters

①

② Click

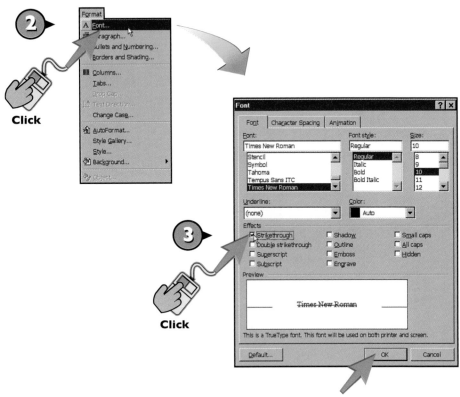

③ Click

Changing the Appearance of Text

You can make text stand out or look special by changing the appearance, or formatting, of the characters. Some of the most commonly used formatting changes—bold, italic, and underline—can be made quickly using the appropriate toolbar buttons. Other changes require selections from the Font dialog box.

① To make text **bold**, *italic*, or <u>underlined</u>, select the text and click the appropriate button on the toolbar. To turn off an attribute, repeat the same steps.

② To apply a different type of formatting, such as strikethrough, click **Format** on the menu bar. Then choose **Font**.

③ In the **Font** dialog box, select the effect you want from the **Font** tab. The Preview area shows you how your text will look. Click **OK** to apply your changes.

 Keyboard Shortcuts
Keyboard shortcuts are **Ctrl+B** for bold, **Ctrl+I** for italic, and **Ctrl+U** for underlined.

Adjusting Line Spacing

Word's default line spacing is set at Single, which means there's exactly enough space to prevent letters from overlapping from line to line, with a little extra to make the lines of text easy to read. However, you can choose other line spacing options to apply, such as Double spacing, or you can specify an exact setting.

 Double-space Tip
Widening the spaces between lines to double space or more is a good idea if you're distributing the rough draft of a document—it provides room for notes.

 Also Known As
Spacing between lines is called *leading*.

Task 9: Changing the Spacing Between Lines

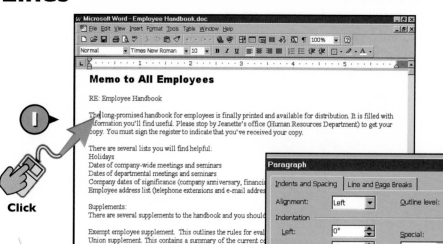

1. Click inside the paragraph you want to change. (For multiple paragraphs, you must select all the paragraphs you want to change.)

2. Open the **Format** menu and choose **Paragraph**.

3. Click the **Line Spacing** drop-down arrow and choose a new value from the list.

4. Click **OK**.

End Task

Task 10: Changing Page Margins

Start Here

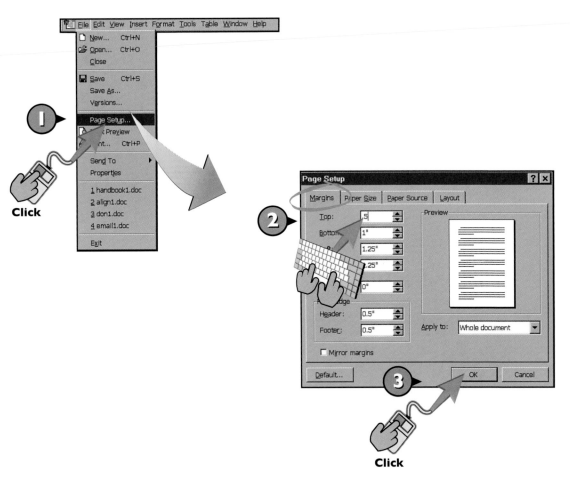

Click

Click

Adjusting Margins

The preset (default) margins for your page can be changed if you either need to fit more text on the page, or need more empty space on the page.

1. Open the **File** menu and choose **Page Setup**.

2. Enter a new number next to each margin you want to change.

3. Click **OK** to apply the new margin settings.

 Letterhead Tip
For printing on letterhead, measure the distance to the company address or logo in inches and set your left or top margin as needed based on the measurement.

End Task

Task 11: Using Undo

Undoing with the Undo Command

When you make a mistake in Word, such as deleting a sentence you didn't mean to or performing a cut and paste that didn't turn out the way you expected, use **Undo** to correct the problem.

✓ **Using the Undo Arrow**
Undo keeps a list of all your actions for each document during your current Word session.

When you select an action from the **Undo** drop-down list, all the actions that occurred after that particular action will also be undone.

You can undo your **Undo** by clicking the **Redo** icon. **Redo** reverses the action of the **Undo** command.

Start Here

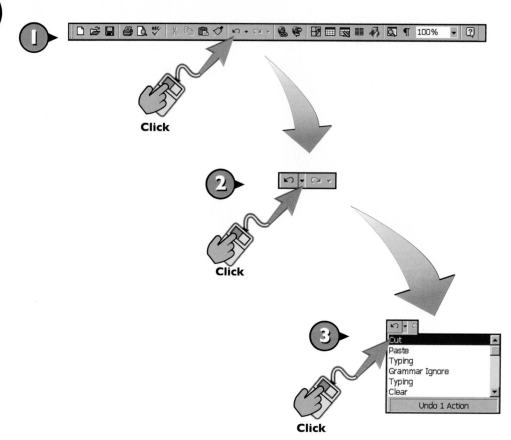

Click

Click

Click

1. After you've done something you want to change, click the **Undo** button to undo that action.

2. If the last action isn't the error you're trying to correct, click the arrow to the right of the **Undo** button to see a list of all your actions.

3. Select the action you want to undo.

End Task

Task 12: Changing the View

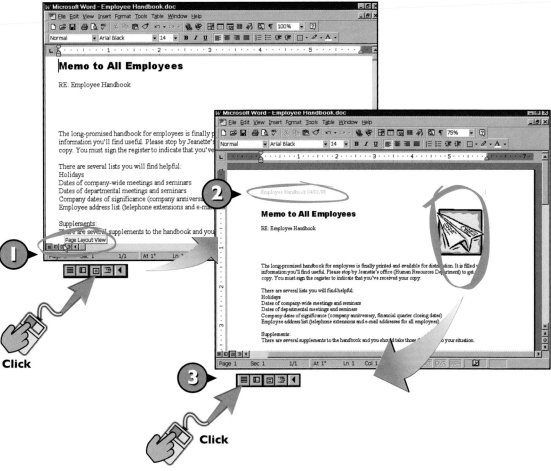

Click

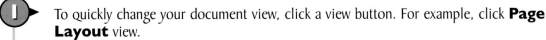

Click

Working with View Options

You can change the way the document appears on your screen with Word's four view options. Each view has its own advantages. The most commonly used views are Normal view and Page Layout view.

✓ **Word's View Options**
Outline view and Online view (for Web documents) should be used only when you're working with those features.

Normal view shows only your formatted text, no graphics or headers and footers, giving you more room to work in your document window.

Page Layout view differs from the Print Preview window in that you can't see several pages at once. To learn more about Print Preview, see Part 1, Task 36.

---

1 To quickly change your document view, click a view button. For example, click **Page Layout** view.

2 Page Layout view shows every element in the document, including graphics, headers, and footers.

3 To return to Normal view again, click the **Normal** view button.

End Task

Task 13: Creating an Outline

Using the Outlining Tools

When you need to prepare long, complicated documents, an outline can usually make it easier to organize your thoughts. Use Word's Outline view to help you arrange your outline's headings, subheadings, and body text. The Outlining toolbar has buttons to help you assign heading levels and view different portions of your outline.

✓ Use the Outlining Buttons

To move text up or down in the outline, select the text and click the **Move Up** or **Move Down** button on the **Outlining** toolbar as many times as needed to move the text to the desired location.

Use the **Expand** and **Collapse** buttons on the toolbar to view or hide subheadings and body text.

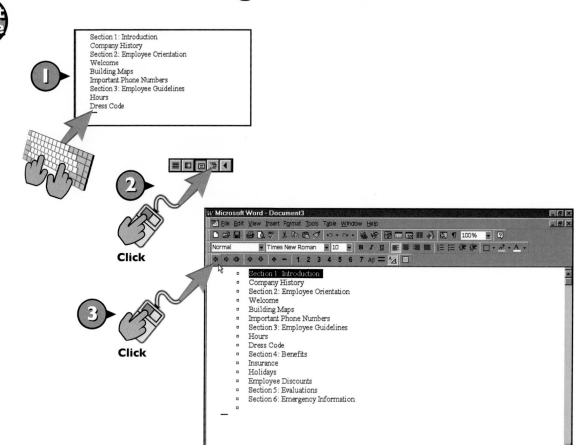

Start Here

Click

Click

1 Type in your outline text and press **Enter** after each heading, subheading, or body text.

2 Click the **Outline** view button to open the document in Outline view.

3 To promote a heading to another level, select the heading and click the **Promote** button.

Next Step

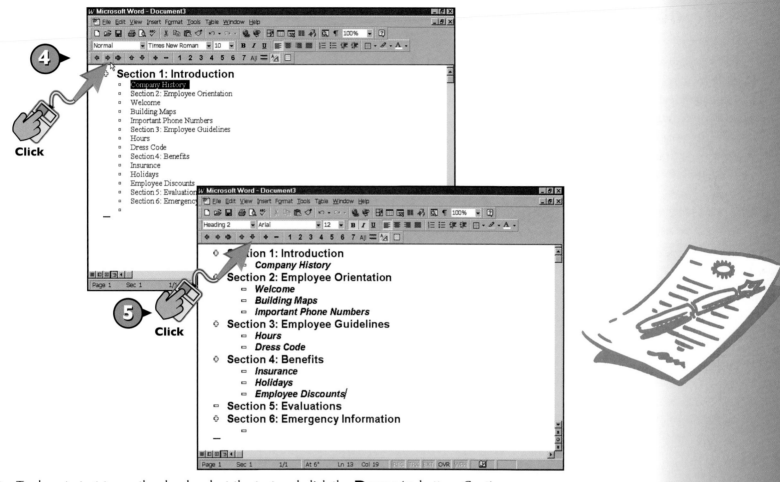

Click

Click

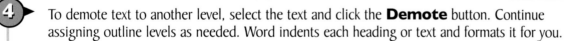

④ To demote text to another level, select the text and click the **Demote** button. Continue assigning outline levels as needed. Word indents each heading or text and formats it for you.

⑤ To demote or promote an entry, select it and use the arrows on the toolbar to make the adjustment (everything below the entry is moved also).

Task 14: Viewing Outline Documents

Working with Outline Levels

Outlines can grow quite large. They can be long and multileveled and consequently overwhelming. Sometimes you need to view only particular levels to make sure everything is where you want it. Other times, you may want to look at one or two additional levels to get a sense of the contents.

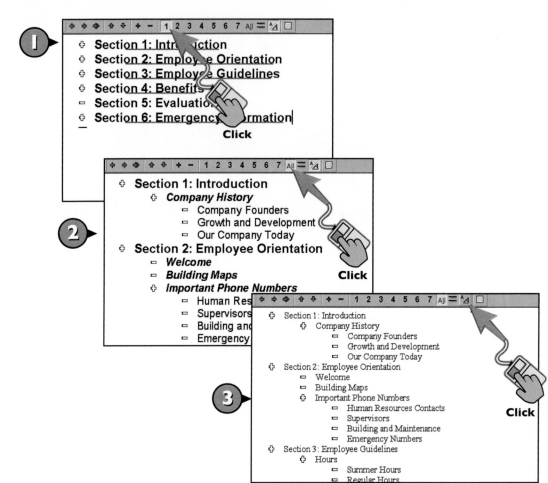

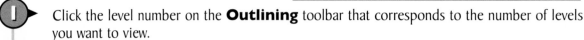

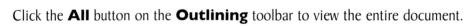

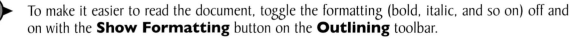

✅ **Use Outline View**
Make sure you're in Outline view (click the **Outline view button**) to see your outline levels and use the **Outlining** toolbar buttons.

1. Click the level number on the **Outlining** toolbar that corresponds to the number of levels you want to view.

2. Click the **All** button on the **Outlining** toolbar to view the entire document.

3. To make it easier to read the document, toggle the formatting (bold, italic, and so on) off and on with the **Show Formatting** button on the **Outlining** toolbar.

Task 15: Applying a Style

Start Here

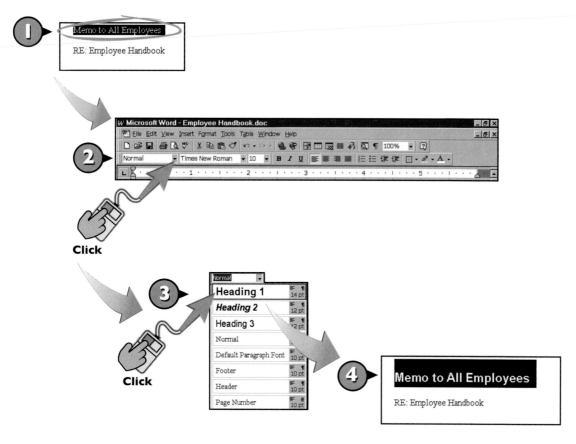

Click

Click

Working with Styles

A *style* is a collection of preset formatting attributes, including font, size, appearance, alignment, and so on. Using styles makes it easy to format a document because all the work is already done for you.

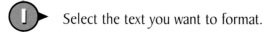
Select the text you want to format.

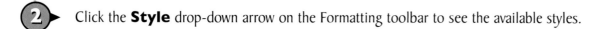
Click the **Style** drop-down arrow on the Formatting toolbar to see the available styles.

3 Choose a new style.

4 Selected text changes to match the formatting for that style.

 Quick Undo
Don't like the style you just assigned? Click the **Undo** button on the Standard toolbar to undo the action.

End Task

Task 16: Changing a Style

Customizing Styles

After you apply a style, you might want to make a small change to its formatting. Perhaps the font or size is wrong, or you want to add another formatting element. You can easily modify Word's styles and save them for future use.

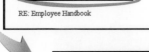

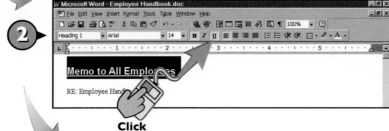

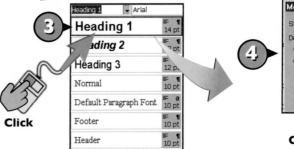

✓ Make Your Own

You can create your own styles from scratch. Open the **Format** menu and choose **Style**. In the Style dialog box, click the **New** button. Type a name for your style in the **Name** box. Use the **Format** button to assign formatting to the style, such as **Font** or **Paragraph** formatting. Click **OK** and then click **Close**. The new style is added to the styles list.

1 ▶ Select the text that uses the style you want to modify.

2 ▶ Make the required formatting change (in this example, **Underline** is being applied).

3 ▶ Click the **Style** drop-down arrow and select the style again.

4 ▶ The Modify Style dialog box opens to ask if you want to change the style. Click **OK** to make the change permanent for this style.

Task 17: Attaching a Template to an Existing Document

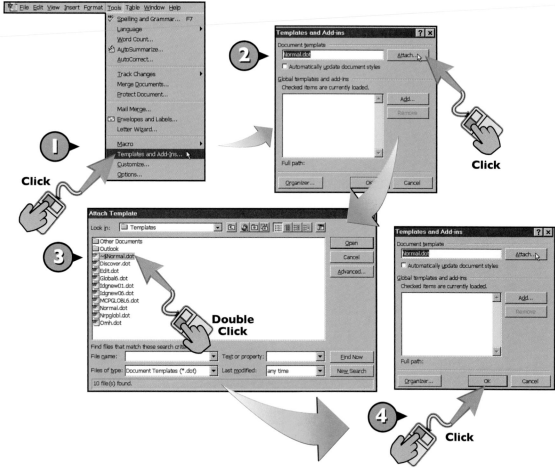

Click

Click

Double Click

Click

Working with Templates

A *template* is a collection of styles, macros, customized toolbars, and other Word features. By default, Word assigns the Normal template to every new document you create unless you specify otherwise. Word comes with other templates you can use. You can also create templates and share them with other users. If you have additional templates available, you can easily attach them to your existing documents.

(1)▶ With your document displayed, open the **Tools** menu and choose **Templates and Add-Ins**.

(2)▶ In the Templates and Add-ins dialog box, choose **Attach**.

(3)▶ When the list of templates displays in the Attach Template dialog box, double-click the template you want to use.

(4)▶ Choose **OK** to exit the dialog box, and the template is attached.

✓ What About the New Button?

If you use the **New** button on the toolbar to begin a new document, you must use these steps to attach a particular template if you want to use something other than the default Normal template.

Basing a New File on a Template

To open a new document based on a template other than the default Normal template, you must use Word's **File, New** command. This opens the New dialog box and lets you preview and choose the template you want to base your document on.

Task 18: Choosing a Template for a New Document

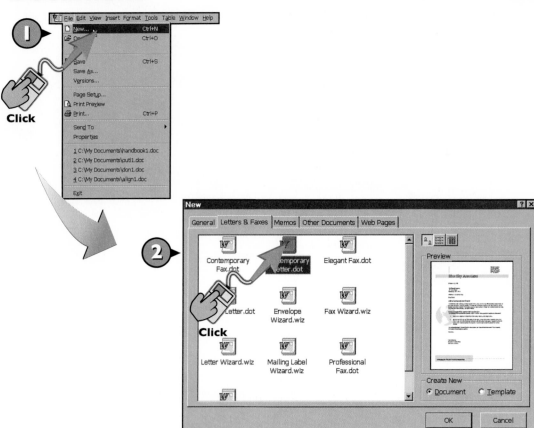

Click

✓ Not the New Button!

If you begin a new document by clicking the **New** button on the Standard toolbar, Word will automatically attach the Normal template. If you want another template applied, you must use the File, New command.

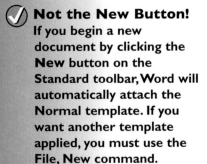

1. Open the **File** menu and choose **New**.

2. In the New dialog box, click the template you want to use. The Preview area shows what the template looks like.

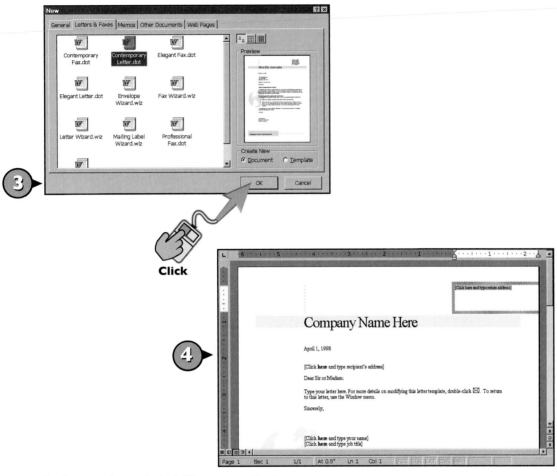

Click

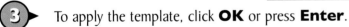

③ To apply the template, click **OK** or press **Enter**.

④ The template opens onscreen ready for you to enter your own text.

✓ **Using Templates with Existing Documents**
To apply a template to an existing document (one you've already created and saved) see Part 1, Task 17, "Attaching a Template to an Existing Document."

✓ **Check It Out!**
Use the tabs in the New dialog box to look through Word's many premade templates. You'll find more templates to add to the lists in the Small Business ValuPack on the Office 97 Small Business Edition CD.

Task 19: Creating an Instant Table

Using the Insert Table Command

You can easily add tables to organize text. Word's Standard toolbar has a shortcut for quickly inserting tables into your documents. The **Insert Table** button lets you quickly define how many rows and columns the table is to have, then immediately creates the table for you.

✓ **Need a Bigger Table?**
Dragging a table using the Insert Table feature limits the table's original size to the width and height your screen permits. If needed, you can add rows and columns later via the **Table** menu commands.

✓ **Quick Format**
After you create a table, you can use the **Table AutoFormat** command on the **Table** menu to customize the appearance of the table.

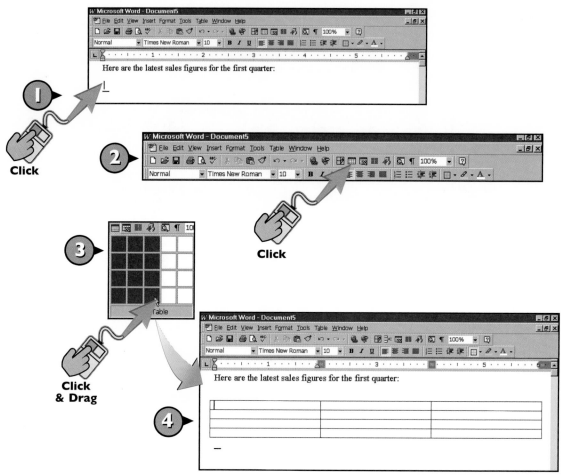

Start Here

Click

Click

Click & Drag

1 Click the location in the document where you want the table to appear.

2 Click the **Insert Table** button on the toolbar.

3 Press and hold the **left mouse button** as you drag down and to the right to select the number of columns and rows you need.

4 Release the mouse button, and the table is placed in your document. Your insertion point is in the first row of the first column, waiting for you to begin entering data.

End Task

Task 20: Creating a Table with the Insert Table Dialog Box

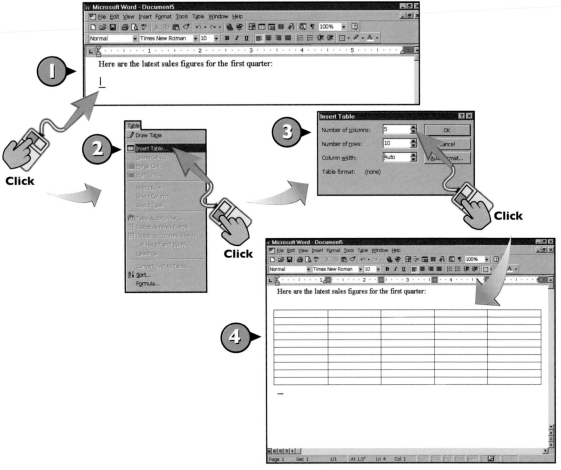

Click

Click

Click

Defining the Table Structure

Word's tables are a perfect way to present text in an organized fashion. When you need to carefully define a table's structure, such as an exact number of rows or columns and the column width, use Word's Insert Table dialog box to help you.

1 ▸ Click the place in your document where you want to insert the table.

2 ▸ Open the **Table** menu and choose **Insert Table**.

3 ▸ Specify the number of columns and rows you need. You can enter the numbers directly, or use the arrows to change the default specifications.

4 ▸ Click **OK**. The table appears in your document as specified.

✓ Quick Format
To learn how to quickly format a table with Word's Table AutoFormat feature, see Part 1, Task 21, "Formatting Tables."

End Task

Task 21: Formatting Tables

Changing Your Table's Appearance

Rather than format your table yourself, why not apply one of Word's AutoFormats instead? You'll save time and effort. You have plenty of formatting styles to choose from, including those that add shading, borders, and grid lines to your table.

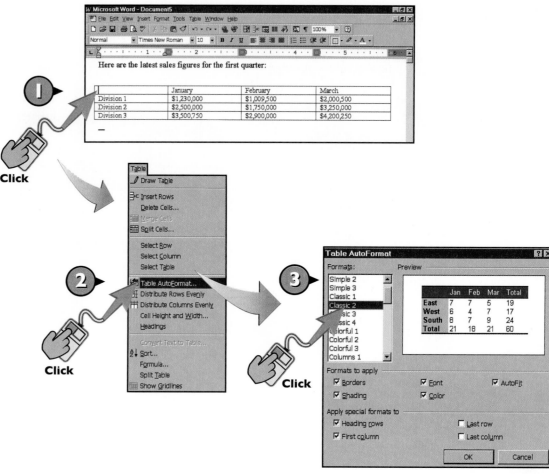

✓ Scroll for More
Use the scroll arrows in the Formats list to see how many formats are available in the Table AutoFormat dialog box.

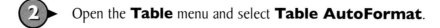

1 ► Click inside the table you want to format (click in any cell).

2 ► Open the **Table** menu and select **Table AutoFormat**.

3 ► From the **Formats** list, select a table format.

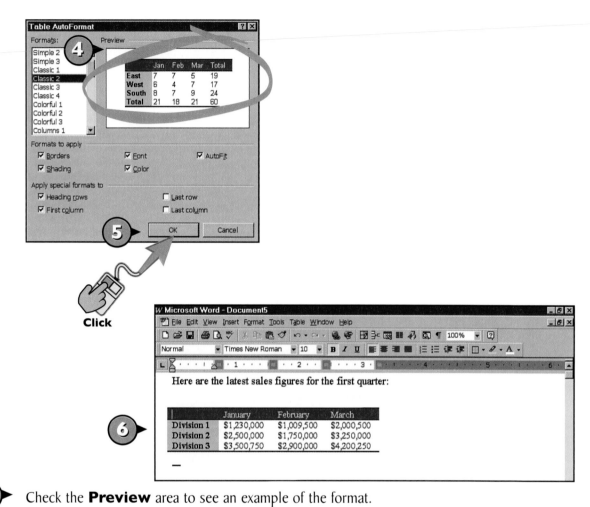

Click

4 Check the **Preview** area to see an example of the format.

5 When you find a format you like, click **OK**.

6 The format is applied to your table.

Task 22: Creating a Numbered List

Using the Numbering Command

Numbered lists are commonly used in documents of all kinds. When you're ready to use a numbered list, use Word's Numbering feature to quickly turn existing text into a neat list.

✓ On or Off
The Numbering toolbar button toggles on or off, so you can select it to turn the feature on and unselect it to turn numbering off.

✓ Customizing Numbers
If you prefer another type of number format for your list, open the **Format** menu and select **Bullets and Numbering**. From the Numbered tab, select another number list style and click **OK**.

✓ Adding Blank Lines
To separate the items in a numbered list with a blank line, press **Shift+Enter** at the end of each list item.

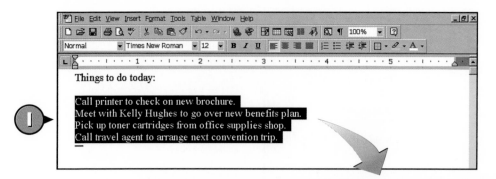

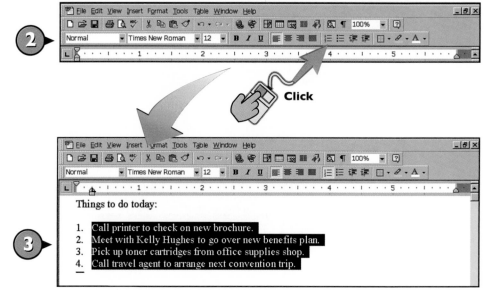

Click

1 To turn existing text into a numbered list, start by selecting the text.

2 Click the **Numbering** button on the toolbar.

3 The text is immediately converted into a numbered list.

End Task

Task 23: Creating a Bulleted List

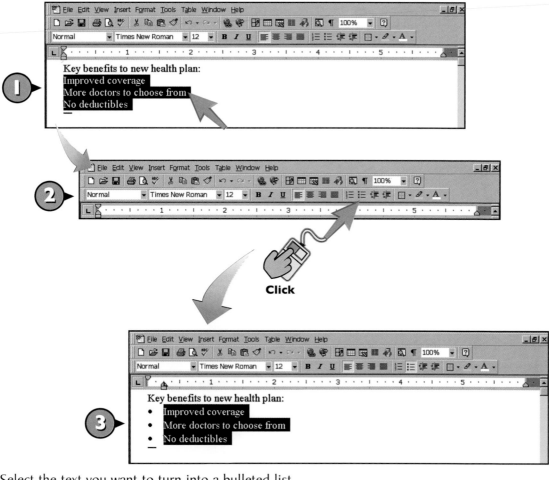

Click

Using the Bullets Command

One of the best ways to draw attention to information is with bullets. A bulleted list really stands out and makes the reader aware of important text. Word's Bullets feature makes creating bulleted lists quite simple.

① Select the text you want to turn into a bulleted list.

② Click the **Bullets** button on the toolbar.

③ The text immediately turns into a bulleted list.

✓ On or Off
The **Bullets** toolbar button toggles on or off, so you can select it to turn the feature on and unselect it to turn bullets off.

✓ Changing the Bullet Format
If you prefer another type of bullet format for your list, open the **Format** menu and select **Bullets and Numbering**. From the **Bulleted** tab, select another bullet style and click **OK**.

Task 24: Adding Headers or Footers

What Are Headers and Footers?

Use headers and footers to place recurring text, such as a title or time and date, at the top or bottom of every page of your document. You only have to enter the text once, then Word takes care of placing it on every page. Fields, which are holding places for information that is updated automatically, can also be placed in a header or a footer. The most commonly used field is the page number.

 Use Page Layout View
After adding a header or footer to your document, be sure to switch to Page Layout view to see the text. You can't see headers or footers in Normal view.

 Use the View Buttons
To quickly change views in Word, use the **View** buttons located to the left of the horizontal scroll bar in the lower-left corner of the screen.

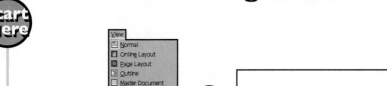

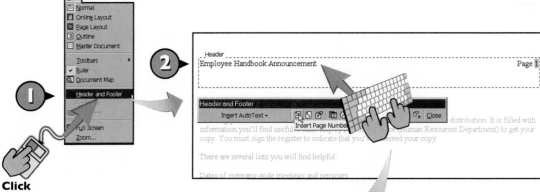

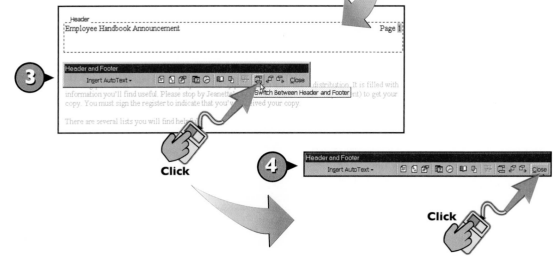

1 To add a header or footer to your document, open the **View** menu and choose **Header and Footer**. Word switches to Page Layout view and opens the Header and Footer toolbar.

2 The cursor is already in place in the Header area. Enter the text you want to use in the header, and also use any of the fields available on the toolbar.

3 If you want to use a footer in addition to, or instead of, a header, click the **Switch Between Header and Footer** button on the toolbar.

4 When you have finished entering text and fields for your header and/or footer, choose **Close** to return to your document.

End Task

Task 25: Inserting an Excel Spreadsheet

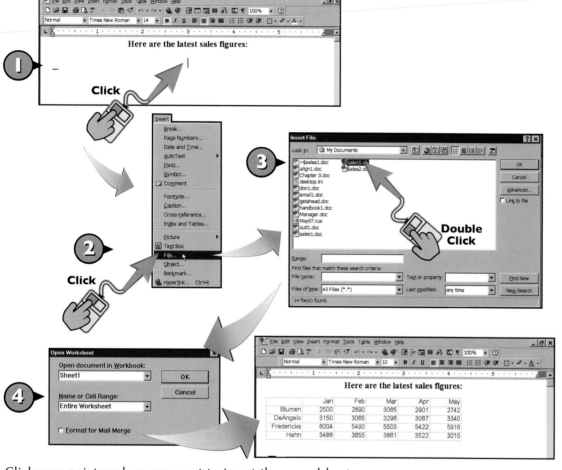

Click

Click

3

Double Click

4

1

Importing Excel Data into Word

If you're working on a report that includes financial data or other information that exists in an Excel Spreadsheet, you can bring the spreadsheet into your document.

1 ► Click your pointer where you want to insert the spreadsheet.

2 ► Open the **Insert** menu and select **File**.

3 ► Locate the folder in which you keep your Excel files and double-click the file you need. (If the **Files of type** box specifies Word documents, change it to **All Files**).

4 ► Choose the appropriate **Sheet** or **Name Range**, then choose **OK**. The spreadsheet data is inserted in your document.

✓ Inserting Ranges
If the spreadsheet is very large, and you've named ranges within the worksheet, you can choose a specific range to insert into Word. Use the **Name or Cell Range** drop-down list in the Open Worksheet dialog box to specify the range you want to use. (See Part 2, Task 17, "Naming a Range of Cells," to learn more about worksheet range names.)

End Task

Task 26: Opening an Existing Document

Using the Open Command

If you have to do more work on an existing document, you have several methods of fetching it and placing it in your Word window.

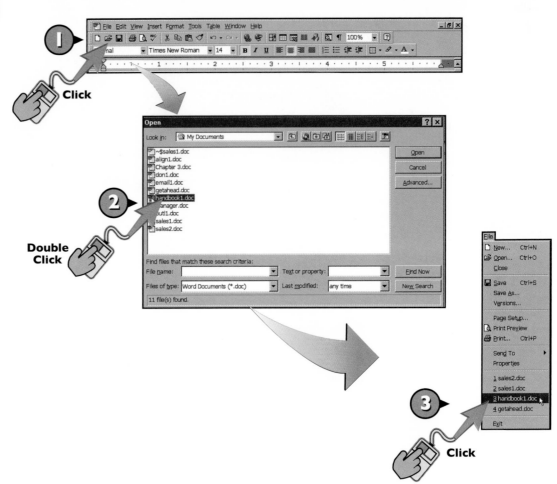

Start Here

Click

Double Click

Click

(✓) **Revisit Recent Files**
Word keeps track of the names of the last four files you worked on and lists them at the bottom of the File menu.

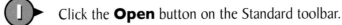
1 Click the **Open** button on the Standard toolbar.

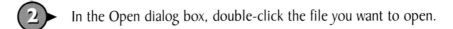
2 In the Open dialog box, double-click the file you want to open.

3 Another way to open a recently worked on file is to display the **File** menu and select the file's name from the bottom of the menu.

End Task

Task 27: Saving Documents

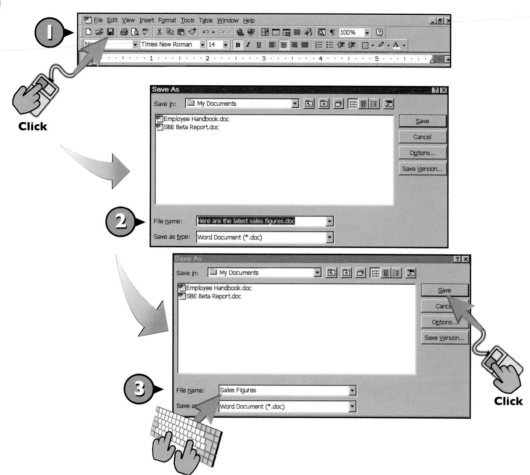

Start Here

Click

Using the Save Command

It's important to save your document soon after you start working on it, and continue to save it frequently. That way, if there's a power loss, your computer freezes, or something else awful occurs, you'll lose only the work you did since the last time you saved.

✓ **Quick Save**
To save changes made to an existing file, click the Save button.

✓ **Changing Folders and Formats**
Use the Save As dialog box to save your file to a specific folder or disk. You can also specify a different file type to save as by using the **Save As Type** drop-down list.

✓ **File Naming Rules**
You can use as many as 255 characters in a filename, including spaces. Filenames can be upper- or lowercase.

1 Click the **Save** button on the Standard toolbar.

2 The first time you save a document, the Save As dialog box opens. Word uses the text at the beginning of the document to guess at a filename, but you'll probably use a better name.

3 Type in the name of the document in the **File name** text box, then click **Save**.

End Task

Task 28: Using Save As

Saving Existing Documents Under New Names

You may want to save a document with a different filename, but keep the original document intact. For example, you may have a letter you've created for one recipient that you also want to send to someone else. Use Word's **Save As** command to create a duplicate file that you can make changes to and save as a different filename.

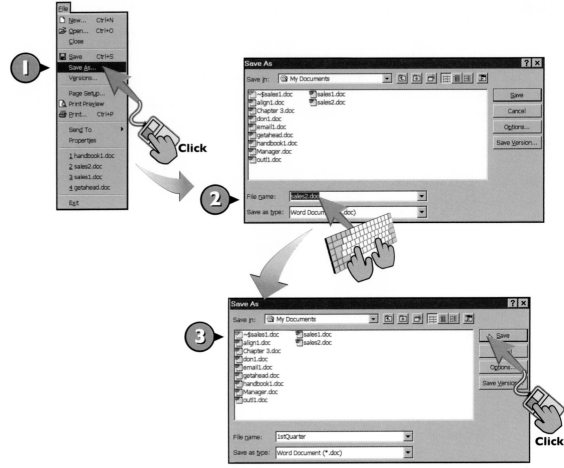

✓ **Changing Folders**
Use the Save As dialog box to save the file to another folder or disk, or specify a different file type.

✓ **File Naming Rules**
When you rename a file, you can use any characters except the same ones used by the original filename.

1 Open the **File** menu and choose **Save As**.

2 The original filename is highlighted in the **File Name** box. Type a new name for the file in the **File Name** box. (You don't have to type the period or the extension "doc".)

3 Click **Save**. The document's title bar now reflects the new name you assigned.

Task 29: Correcting Spelling as You Work

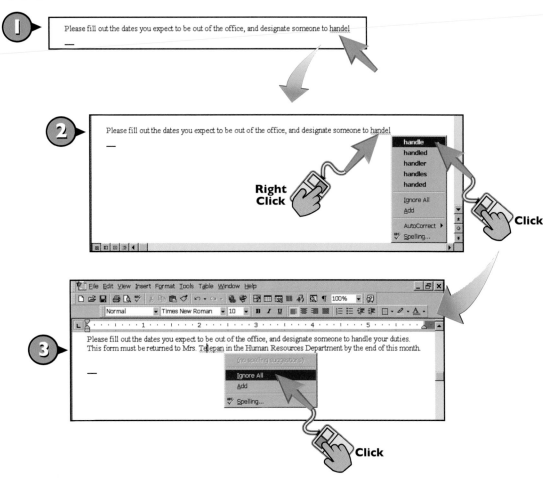

① Please fill out the dates you expect to be out of the office, and designate someone to handel

② Please fill out the dates you expect to be out of the office, and designate someone to handel

handle
handled
handler
handles
handed

Ignore All
Add

AutoCorrect ▶
Spelling...

Right Click

Click

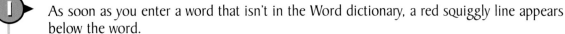

③ File Edit View Insert Format Tools Table Window Help

Normal Times New Roman 10 B I U

Please fill out the dates you expect to be out of the office, and designate someone to handle your duties. This form must be returned to Mrs. Telepan in the Human Resources Department by the end of this month.

(no spelling suggestions)

Ignore All
Add

Spelling...

Click

① As soon as you enter a word that isn't in the Word dictionary, a red squiggly line appears below the word.

② Right-click on the word and click the correct spelling from the list that's presented. Word automatically changes the spelling for you.

③ If the word is a proper name, you can choose **Ignore All** so it won't be considered a mistake in the future.

Using Word's Spell Check Feature

Word automatically checks your spelling as you work, giving you an opportunity to stay accurate without having to go through a spell check of the entire document after it's finished.

✓ **Turning Off Automatic Spell Check**
You can turn off automatic spell check by choosing **Tools, Options** and removing the check mark next to **Check Spelling As You Type** in the Spelling & Grammar tab.

✓ **It's a Limited Dictionary**
Word's dictionary isn't totally comprehensive, so you may find the automatic spell check underlining proper nouns that are actually spelled correctly.

End Task

Using the Grammar Check Tool

If you make a grammar error, or write a sentence that could stand some expert tweaking, Word points it out with a green squiggly underline. You can edit the error directly yourself, or you can see what Word's Grammar check suggests. If it's a serious grammar error, of course, you should correct it one way or another.

✓ **Turning Off Grammar Check**
You can turn off automatic grammar checking by opening the **Tools** menu, and choosing **Options**. Deselect the **Check Grammar As You Type** option in the Spelling & Grammar tab.

✓ **What Fragment?**
If you right-click over a grammar error and see Fragment (no suggestion), this usually means you're missing a verb.

Task 30: Correcting Grammar as You Work

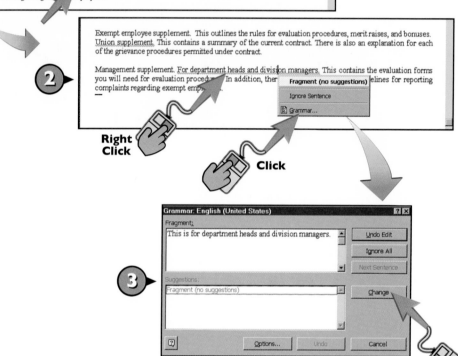

 When a sentence needs attention, a green squiggly line appears below it.

 Right-click anywhere in the sentence to see what the grammar checker has to say. Choose **Grammar** to open the Grammar dialog box.

 Edit the sentence, and then choose **Change** to replace the sentence with your edited version. (Click **Close** to exit the Grammar dialog box.)

Task 31: Running Spell Check

Start Here

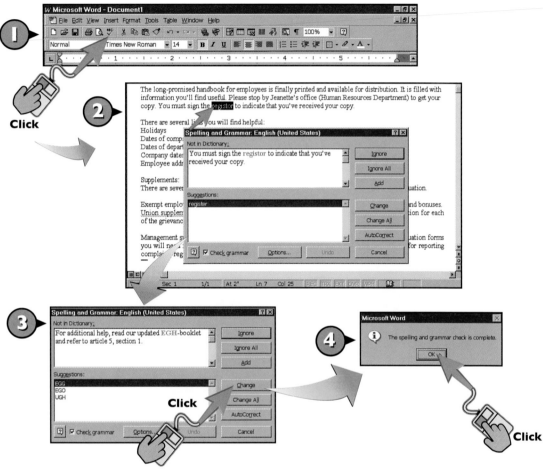

Click

Performing a Spell Check

It's a good idea to run Word's spell check feature before you print a finished file (especially if you've turned off the automatic spell check). A spell check checks your text against Word's dictionary to find obvious misspellings.

✓ **It's Not Misspelled!**
Word's dictionary isn't totally comprehensive, so you may find that spell check points out proper nouns as misspellings even though you know they're spelled correctly. Choose **Ignore All** to skip the error or, if you want to include the term as part of the dictionary, click the **Add** button.

1. Click the **Spelling and Grammar** button on the Standard toolbar.

2. The checker stops at the first mistake it finds, highlighting it in the text and opening the Spelling and Grammar dialog box.

3. Select a suggested spelling (there may be only one) and choose **Change**. Or, choose **Ignore** or **Add** to tell the spell checker how to handle proper names and technical terms.

4. The spell checker moves on to the next mistake. Continue to make adjustments until the entire document is totally checked. When the spell check is complete, click **OK**.

✓ **Turn Grammar Check Off**
Want to check spelling only and not grammar? Deselect the **Check grammar** check box in Spelling and Grammar dialog box.

End Task

Task 32: Using AutoCorrect

Working with AutoCorrect

Word has gathered a list of commonly misspelled words (many of them due to typing errors) and uses the list to make automatic corrections as you type. For example, if you accidentally type "hte," AutoCorrect automatically changes the spelling to "the" for you. You can create your own AutoCorrect entries or change the ones Word has stored.

✅ **AutoCorrect Tip**

Enter shortcuts for long technical terms or names to have AutoCorrect save you some typing. For example, if you constantly need to type in your company's name, create an AutoCorrect entry for it so you only have to type one or two letters, and the entire name is inserted for you.

✅ **Turn It Off!**

To turn AutoCorrect off, choose **Tools, Auto-Correct** and deselect the **Replace Text As You Type** check box.

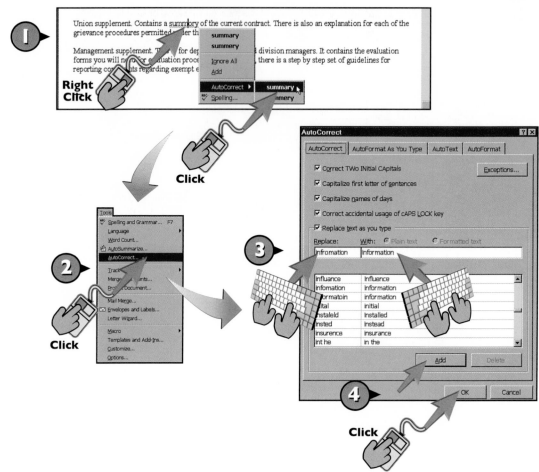

I If automatic spell check catches a word you misspell frequently, add it to the AutoCorrect list. Right-click the word, select **AutoCorrect**, then select the correct spelling from the submenu.

2 To add your own AutoCorrect entries to the AutoCorrect list, choose **Tools, AutoCorrect**.

3 Enter the word you frequently type incorrectly into the **Replace** text box, and then enter its correct spelling in the **With** text box.

4 Choose **Add**, and then choose **OK**.

Task 33: Using the Thesaurus

Start Here

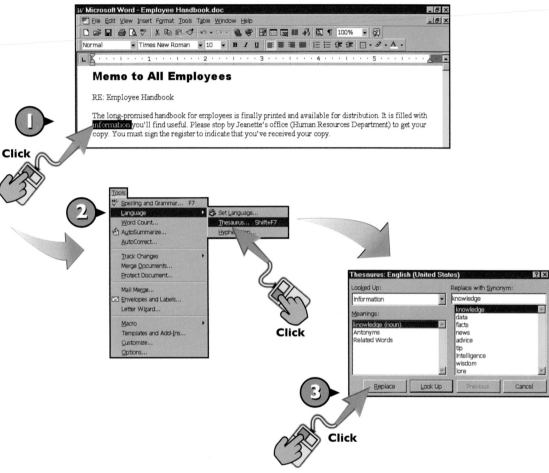

Click

Click

Click

End Task

Working with Word's Thesaurus

You can tap into Word's Thesaurus tool to help you with the writing of your documents. Using the Thesaurus, you can look up words, including synonyms and antonyms, and replace your text with words that better express your thoughts.

① Select the word you want to replace.

② Open the **Tools** menu and select **Language**, then **Thesaurus**. The Thesaurus opens with a list of synonyms displayed.

③ Select the word you want to use to replace your original word, and then click **Replace.**

✓ **Look Up Words**
You can use the Thesaurus to look up words. From the Thesaurus dialog box, type the word you want to look up in the **Replace with Synonym** text box, and then click the **Look Up** button. Use the **Meanings** list box to look up related words or antonyms.

Task 34: Finding Text

Searching Your Document

Use Word's Find command to look up words or phrases in your document. If you have a particularly long document, the Find feature can help you quickly locate the text you're looking for without having to scroll and search by reading the entire document.

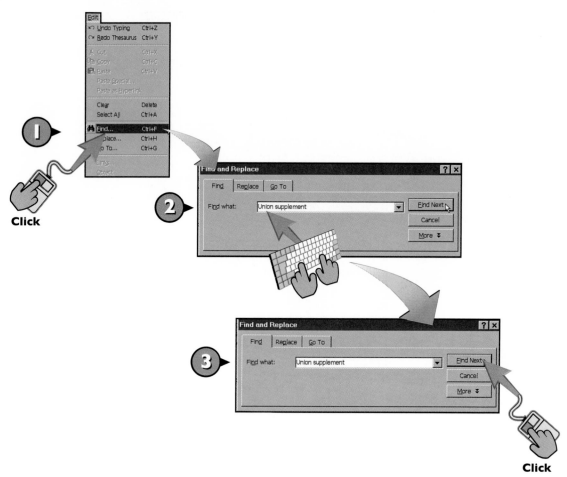

Click

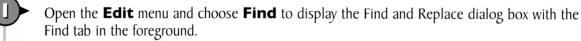

Click

✓ More Options

If you want to look for uppercase words or match the case exactly, use the **More** button in the Find and Replace dialog box to display additional options you can use as you search for words.

1 ▶ Open the **Edit** menu and choose **Find** to display the Find and Replace dialog box with the Find tab in the foreground.

2 ▶ Enter the word or phrase you want to find.

3 ▶ Choose **Find Next**.

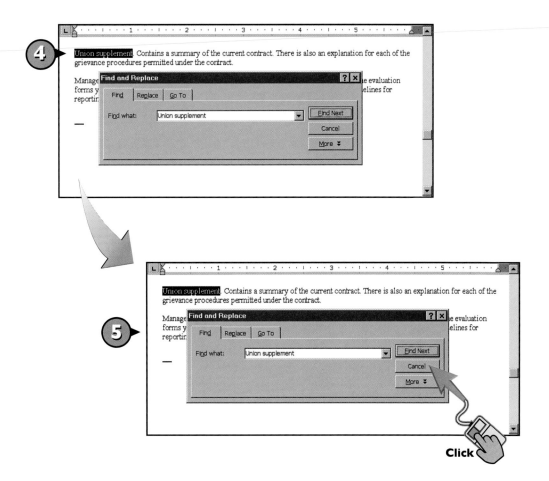

Click

④ Word moves you to the next occurrence of the word(s) you entered.

⑤ Choose **Cancel** to close the dialog box and work on your document. Choose **Find Next** if this isn't the right spot and you want to move to the next occurrence of the word(s).

Task 35: Using Replace

Working with the Replace Feature

Use Word's Replace feature to look up words in your document and replace them with new text. For example, if you type a five-page report and find you misspelled someone's name, use the Replace command to fix your mistakes quickly without having to scroll and search your entire document. You can choose to replace each occurrence of the word, or every occurrence in the entire document.

Start Here

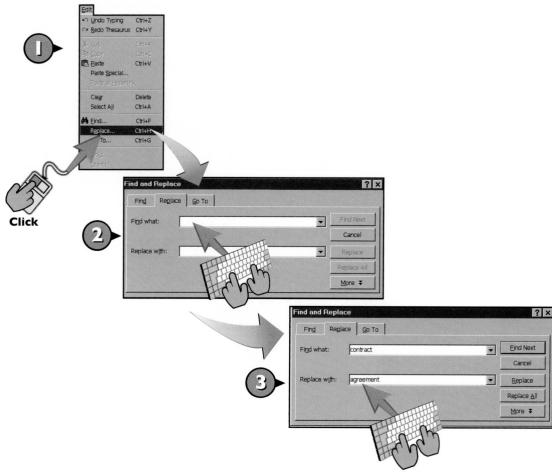

Click

✓ Using Replace All

If you're absolutely sure that you want to replace every occurrence of a word (perhaps you spelled Mr. Smythe's name as Smith), choose **Replace All** in the dialog box.

1 ▶ Open the **Edit** menu and select **Replace**.

2 ▶ In the open Find and Replace dialog box, type in the word you want to get rid of in the **Find What** box.

3 ▶ Click inside the **Replace With** box and enter the replacement word.

Next Step

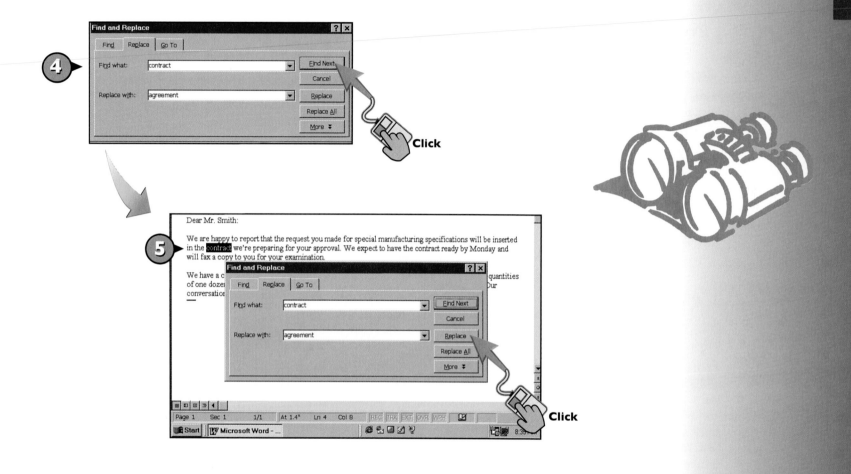

Click

Click

<table>
<tr><td>4</td><td>Click on Find Next to move to the next occurrence of the word in your document.</td></tr>
</table>

4 ▸ Click on **Find Next** to move to the next occurrence of the word in your document.

5 ▸ Choose **Replace** to make the substitution. Word moves to the next occurrence of the word.
If you don't want to make the change, choose **Find Next** to move to the next occurrence.

End Task

Task 36: Previewing the Printed Page

Using the Preview Window

Previewing how your page will look before you print it is always a good idea. By previewing the document, you can see if any special formatting or graphics need adjusting.

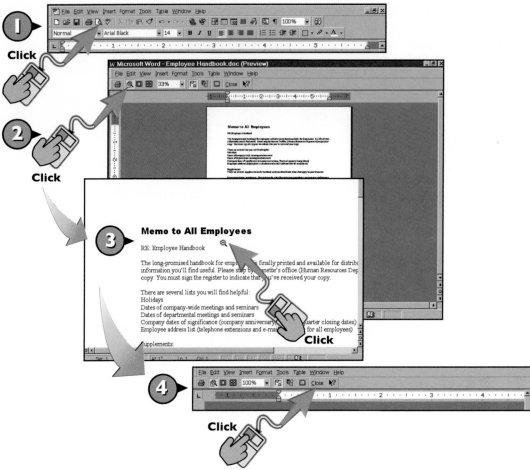

✓ **Editing from Preview**
To make edits directly in the Preview window, deselect the **Magnifier** tool and click where you want to edit. You can then make your changes to the text.

✓ **Measure with the Rulers**
Notice that the rulers in the Print Preview window show the exact size of your printed page.

1 ▸ Click the **Print Preview** button on the Standard toolbar to open the document in the Print Preview window.

2 ▸ To zoom in on your document, click on the **Magnifier** icon on the Preview toolbar.

3 ▸ Your mouse pointer takes the shape of a magnifying glass. Position it anywhere and click to zoom in on that spot on the page.

4 ▸ When you are finished, choose **Close** to close the Preview window.

End Task

Task 37: Printing a Document

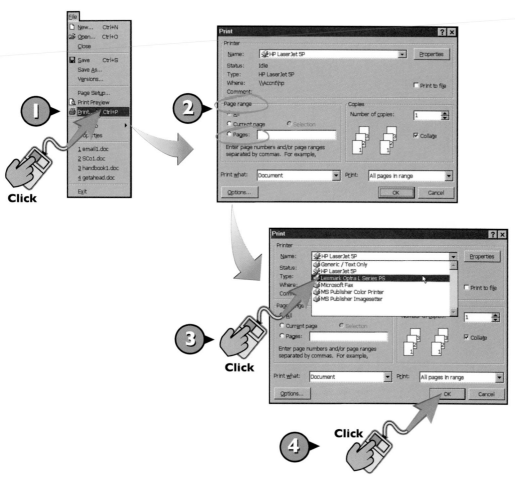

Click

Click

Click

Using the Print Command

After you complete a document, you may want to print it for mailing, distribution, or filing. The computer jargon for a printed document is "hard copy." (The file on your hard drive is called the "soft copy," or the electronic file.)

✓ Quick Print

If you know all the printing settings are correct, click the **Print** button on the toolbar to quickly print the document without seeing the Print dialog box.

✓ Need to Change the Paper Size?

To change your paper orientation or paper size options, click the **Properties** button in the Print dialog box and make the necessary changes.

1 ▶ Open the **File** menu and choose **Print**.

2 ▶ In the Print dialog box, verify that all of the information is correct. You have the option of selecting specific pages, multiple copies, or changing your printer selection.

3 ▶ To choose a different printer, click the **Name** drop-down arrow and use the scroll button to view your options. Click the printer you want to use.

4 ▶ When you are happy with your settings and ready to print, click **OK**.

Task 38: Printing One Page of a Document

Start Here

Using the Page Options

If you want to print only a portion of your document, use the Print dialog box to designate the exact page or selection.

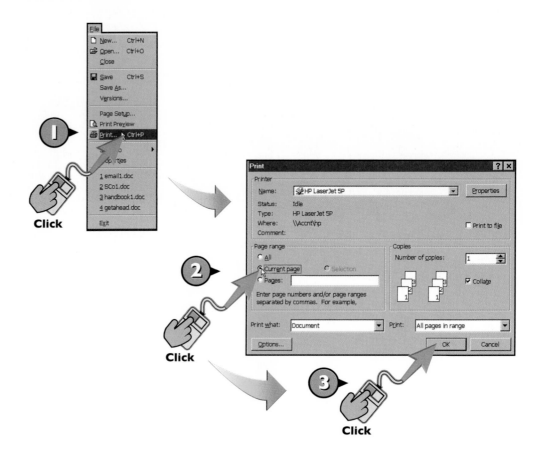

Click

Click

Click

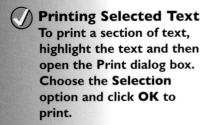
Printing Selected Text
To print a section of text, highlight the text and then open the Print dialog box. Choose the **Selection** option and click **OK** to print.

1 Display the page you want to print in the Word window, then open the **File** menu and choose **Print**.

2 In the Print dialog box, click the **Current Page** option.

3 Choose **OK** to print the page.

End Task

Task 39: Printing a Range of Pages

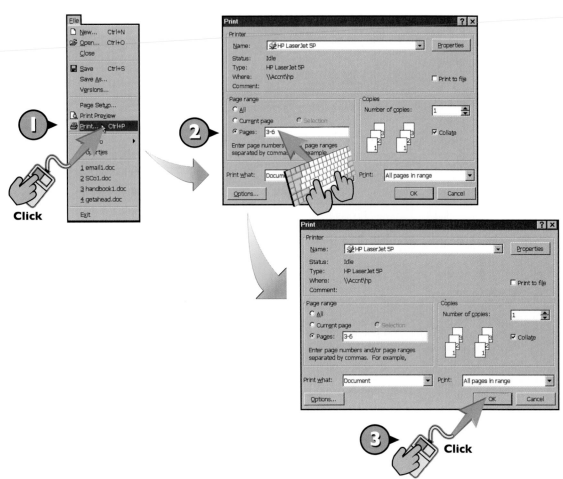

Click

Click

Designating a Print Range

You can print a specific range of pages from a document. This is useful if the document is a large compilation of subjects and each new subject starts on a fresh page. Or, if you made corrections to a document after printing it, you need to print only those pages that need replacing.

① ▶ Open the **File** menu and choose **Print**.

② ▶ In the Print dialog box, select the **Pages** option and enter the range of pages you want to print. For example, **1-3** prints pages 1, 2, and 3.

③ ▶ Click **OK** to print.

✓ Page Tips
To print from a specific page to the end of the document, enter **X-** in the **Pages** text box, substituting the first page you want to print for the **X**.

Print specific noncontiguous pages by separating the page numbers with a comma, such as **2,4** (which prints only pages 2 and 4).

End
Task

Task 40: Printing Selected Text

Using the Selection Option

If you need to print some specific text rather than an entire document, the Print dialog box provides this function.

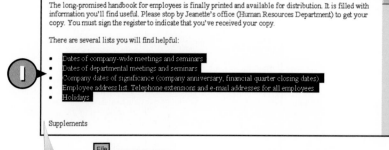

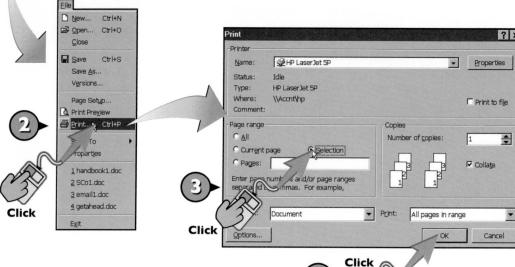

Click

Click

Click

1. Select the text you want to print.

2. Open the **File** menu and choose **Print**.

3. In the Print dialog box, choose **Selection**.

4. Click **OK**, and your printer prints only the selected text.

Task 41: Tracking Revisions

Start Here

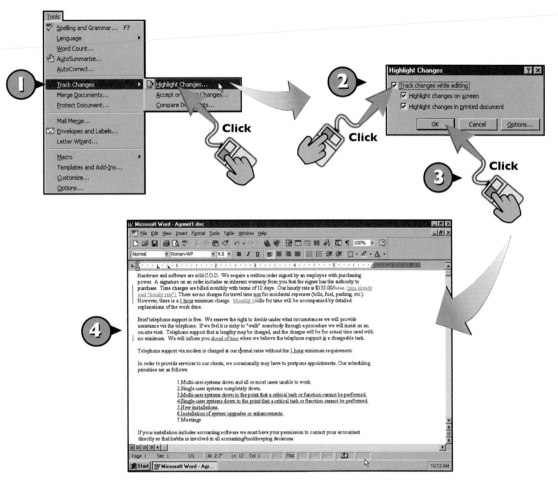

Click

Click

Click

Frequently, an important document such as a contract or a proposal passes through many hands. Everybody concerned wants to make sure that all the important points are covered. You can allow people to add or delete information without permanently changing the text by tracking changes made to a document. (In fact, that's how books like the one you're reading are edited.)

To enable revision tracking, open the **Tools** menu and choose **Track Changes, Highlight Changes**.

Select **Track changes while editing**. Then specify whether you want to see revisions highlighted on the screen, in the printed document, or both.

When you are happy with your settings, choose **OK**.

As each person adds or deletes text, that text appears in a different color. Deletions aren't deleted, just crossed out, so you can see all the changes. Additions are underlined.

Who Did It?
To learn who made a revision, position your pointer over the revised text. The time and date of the change also appears.

End Task

Using the Accept and Reject Commands

After everybody you are working with has made comments and changes on your document, you can decide which revisions you want to accept and which to reject.

Task 42: Accepting and Rejecting Revisions

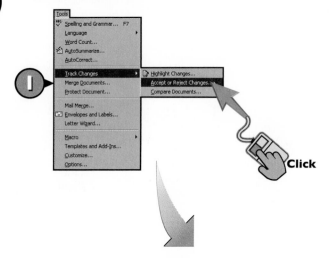

Start Here

Click

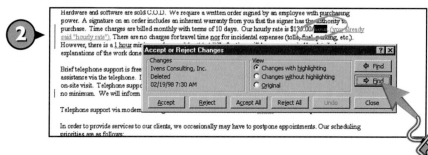

Click

 Accept or Reject All
You can also choose **Accept All** or **Reject All** in the Accept or Reject Changes dialog box to make a sweeping judgment and okay or nix all the revisions without checking each one. Word asks you to confirm the decision; click **Yes.**

I Choose **Tools**, **Track Changes**, **Accept or Reject Changes**.

2 In the Accept or Reject Changes dialog box, choose **Find**. The first revision is highlighted in your text.

 Next Step

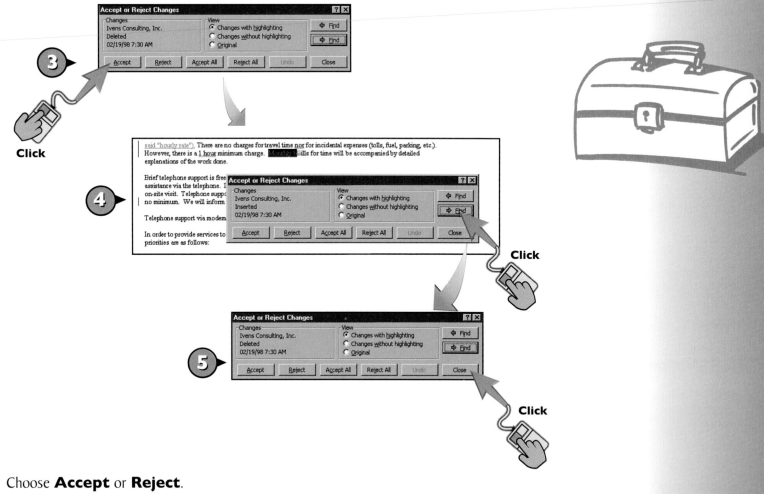

Click

3 ▶ Choose **Accept** or **Reject**.

4 ▶ Press **Find** again and the next revision is highlighted automatically so that you can continue. If you're not sure about a change, choose **Find** to move on to the next revision.

5 ▶ Word prompts you when you're finished finding revisions. Click **OK**, and then click **Close**.

Task 43: Comparing Documents

Comparing Changes

If you want to see the differences between two similar documents, Word provides a tool for you. It's useful if people make changes to your document without turning on the revisions feature (and they thought you wouldn't notice and they could get away with it).

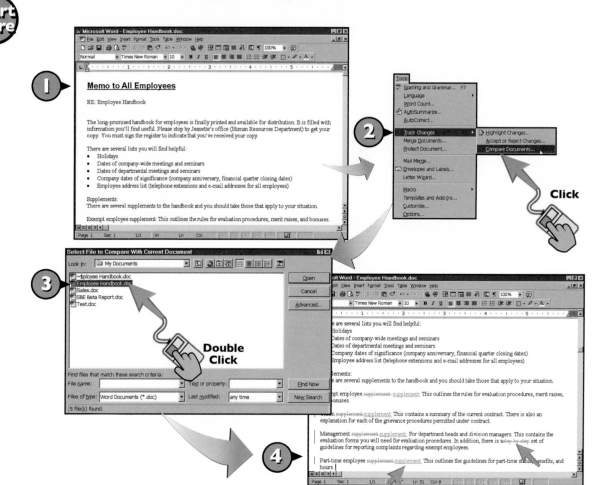

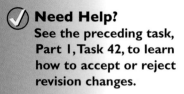

Double Click

✓ Need Help?
See the preceding task, Part 1, Task 42, to learn how to accept or reject revision changes.

1 Open one of the two documents you want to compare.

2 Choose **Tools**, **Track Changes**, **Compare Documents**.

3 The Select File to Compare With Current Document dialog box opens. Double-click the document you want to compare with the one in the Word window.

4 The original document displays revisions to indicate the differences between the documents.

Task 44: Creating and Printing Envelopes

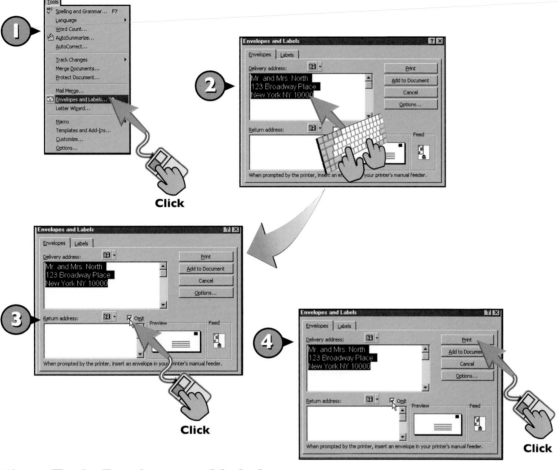

Click

Click

Click

Start Here

Using the Envelopes and Labels Dialog Box

Word has a feature for creating envelopes that's incredibly easy. The only difficulty you'll face is figuring out how to feed the envelopes into your printer.

---

1 ▸ Choose **Tools**, **Envelopes and Labels**.

2 ▸ If you are composing a letter, Word grabs the address for you from the document. Otherwise, enter the address in the **Delivery address** box.

3 ▸ If you are using plain, blank envelopes, enter your address in the **Return address** box. If you use preprinted envelopes, select **Omit**, and Word will remember the setting.

4 ▸ Choose **Print**.

Envelope Tip
If your printer has a back door for straight-through printing, always open it when you print envelopes. Envelopes can drift if they have to make their way around the roller.

End Task

Task 45: Configuring Envelopes

Customizing Envelope Size

Word's default envelope size is for a standard business envelope (size #10 in the world of envelopes jargon), but not all mail goes out in the same size envelope. You may need to designate another size to use. Word's Envelope Options enable you to customize the configuration for envelopes, including choosing envelope size, font, even adding postal bar codes.

 Start Here

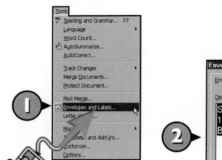

Click

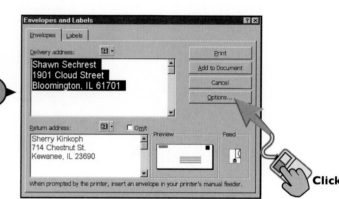

Click

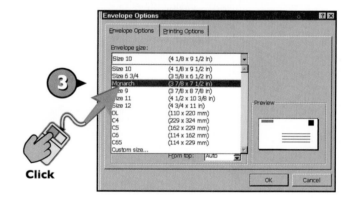

Click

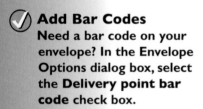 **Add Bar Codes**
Need a bar code on your envelope? In the Envelope Options dialog box, select the **Delivery point bar code** check box.

 Choose **Tools**, **Envelopes and Labels**.

 Click the **Options** button to open the Envelope Options dialog box.

 To change the size of the envelope, click the **Envelope size** drop-down arrow and select a size from the list.

 Next Step

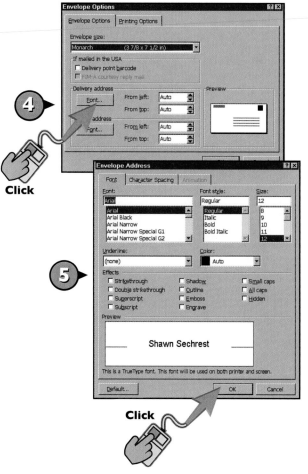

Click

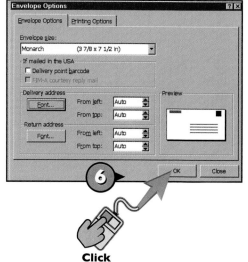

Click

Click

4 To change the font, click the **Font** button.

5 Change the formatting settings as needed, and then click **OK**.

6 Click **OK** to return to the Envelopes and Labels dialog box. Now you're ready to enter an address, if needed, and print the envelope.

✓ **Adjust Margins**
If you need to adjust the margins for printing your addresses on the envelope, you can do that in the Envelope Options dialog box, too. Use the **Delivery Address** and **Return Address** margin fields (**From Left, From Top**) to set new margins. Click on the arrows or enter a margin setting in the appropriate box.

✓ **Printing Help**
See Part 1, Task 44, to learn how to print your envelopes.

Task 46: Viewing Nonprinting Characters

Showing and Hiding Paragraph Marks

When you press the Spacebar, the Enter key, or the Tab key, Word marks the entries and moves your insertion point accordingly. By default, you can't see these marks. However, sometimes it's helpful to see them so you can tell where paragraphs and tabs begin and end.

(✓) **They Won't Print**
If you turn paragraph marks on and print your document, don't worry, the marks won't print.

(✓) **Viewing Specific Characters**
To specify exactly which nonprinting characters you want to view, open the **Tools** menu and select **Options**. Click the **View** tab and select the characters you want to see. Click **OK** to exit the dialog box.

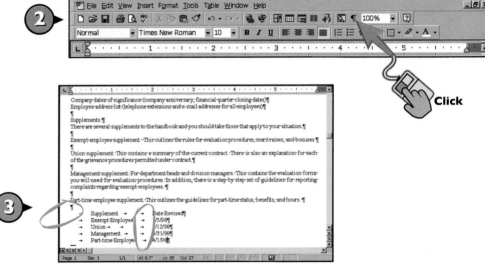

Click

1. Open the document whose nonprinting characters you want to see.

2. Click the **Show/Hide** button on the Standard toolbar.

3. Your document screen displays a symbol for each nonprinting character, such as paragraph and tab marks.

End Task

Task 47: Inserting the Date and Time

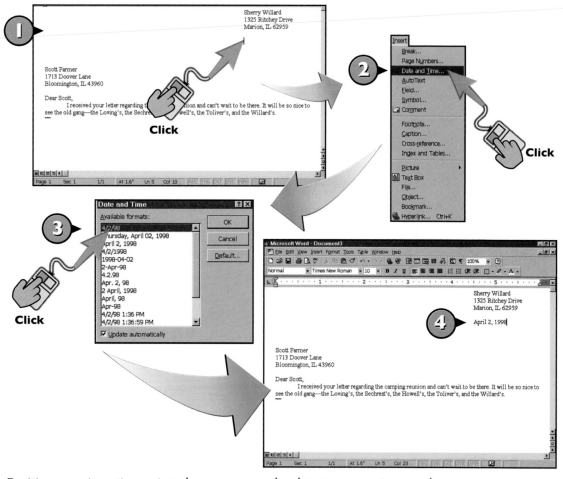

Click

Click

Click

Using Date and Time Codes

Don't type the date on letters; let Word do it for you. You can easily insert the date or time, or both, into any document. You can even insert a code that keeps the date or time current. The next time you open the document, the code will reflect the most current date or time.

✓ **Automatic Updates**
To insert a code that updates the date or time for you whenever you open the document, select the **Update automatically** check box in the Date and Time dialog box.

✓ **Is it Real or Code?**
If you choose to insert a date or time code, you won't be able to tell the difference between characters and code unless you place your insertion point in the text. The code appears as a block, and you won't be able to edit any of the characters it contains.

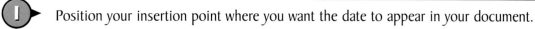

1. Position your insertion point where you want the date to appear in your document.

2. Open the **Insert** menu and select **Date and Time**.

3. Select the format you want to use and click **OK**.

4. The date or time (or both) appear in the document.

End Task

Task 48: Opening Multiple Documents

Working with Two or More Files

You can work on more than one document at a time in Word and use the **Window** menu to switch between the open documents. For instance, you may want to have an outline open as you create a document that follows that outline. Or, perhaps you've recorded some notes for yourself as you prepare a complicated document and want to refer to them occasionally.

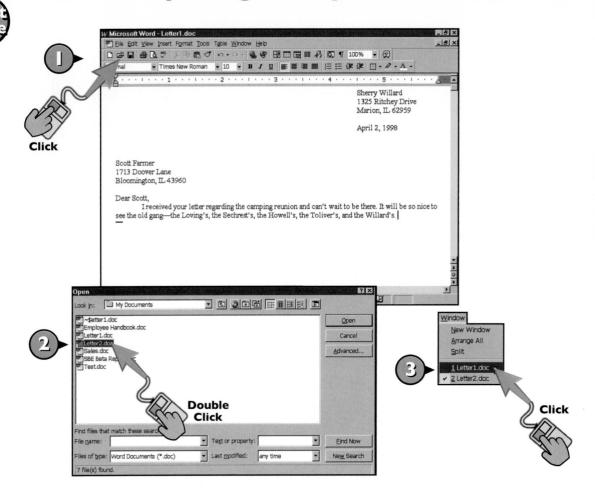

Start Here

Click

Double Click

Click

View Multiple Documents at Once
You can also view your open documents onscreen at the same time. Turn to Part 1, Task 49, to learn how.

 With your first document already opened and displayed in the Word window, click the **Open** button.

 Double-click the document you want to open. (Notice that any currently opened documents are displayed at the top of the list with special characters in front of the filename.)

 Open the **Window** menu and select the document you want to work on (the currently displayed document has a check mark next to its name).

End Task

Task 49: Viewing Multiple Documents

Start Here

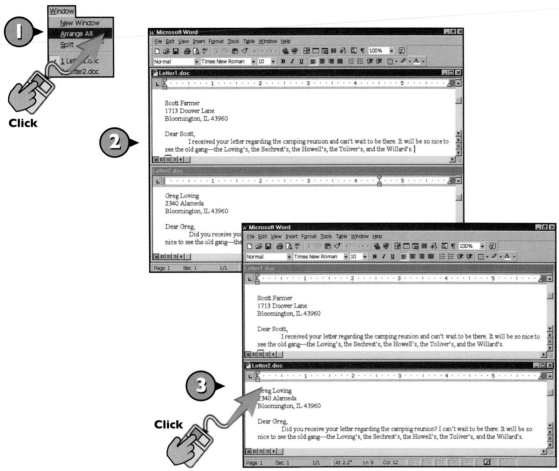

Click

Click

Using the Arrange All Command

When you're working with more than one document at a time and you need to refer to one in order to create the other, it's easier to have them both in view. The drawback is that you have less document space for each, so you see less of the text.

✓ **Which is Active?**
When you have multiple documents on the screen, the active document has a blue title bar and the control buttons appear on the right edge of the title bar. Toolbar buttons and menu commands apply to the active document only.

✓ **Maximize It**
If you are viewing two open documents and decide to close one, the other document remains in a small window—click the **Maximize** button to restore it to full-screen view.

1. Open the **Window** menu and select **Arrange All**.

2. The documents appear as narrow windows onscreen, one on top of another (if you have more than two documents open, there are more narrow windows stacked vertically).

3. Switch between documents by clicking anywhere in the document window that you want to make active.

End Task

Task 50: Moving and Copying Text Between Documents

Start Here

Sharing Data Between Files

It's not unusual to take text from one document and use it in another document. For example, you may have a paragraph in one document that needs to be copied to another, or perhaps you have some sales figures that need to be moved from one report to another. An easy way to do this is to drag the text from one open window to another, providing both documents are onscreen at the same time.

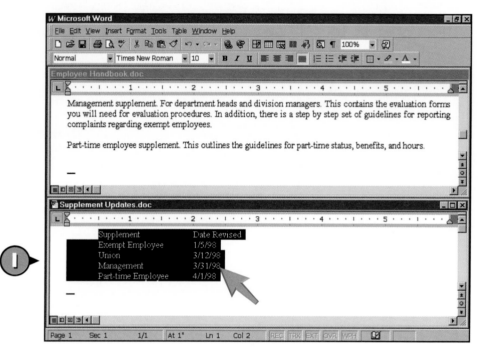

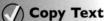 **Copy Text**

The task steps show how to move text, but to copy it instead, hold down the **Ctrl** key while you drag.

1 Select the text you want to move.

Next Step

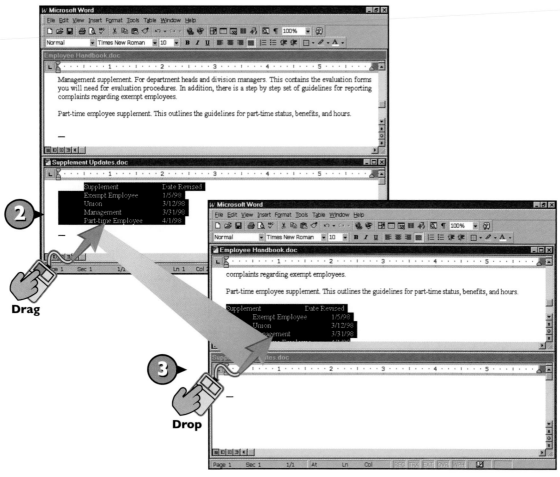

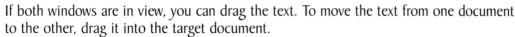

Drag

Drop

✅ **Use the Shortcut Menu**

If you're not viewing both documents onscreen at the same time, but both documents are open, you can still move or copy text between them. Right-click the selected text you want to move or copy and choose **Cut** or **Copy** from the shortcut menu. Then use the **Windows** menu to switch to the other document. Right-click where you want the text inserted and choose **Paste**.

2 ▶ If both windows are in view, you can drag the text. To move the text from one document to the other, drag it into the target document.

3 ▶ Release the mouse button, and the text is inserted in the document.

End Task

PART 2

Excel

Excel is a spreadsheet program designed to specifically help you work with and manipulate numbers. The term "spreadsheet" is an accounting term for the long green- and white-striped ledgers used to record numbers. Although Excel is certainly a great tool for recording numbers and lists, its true strength lies in its mathematical features. Use Excel's built-in formulas, called functions, to perform quick calculations on your data.

Excel is the perfect tool for any small business task involving numbers. You can analyze sales figures, track expenses, build graphs and charts, set up and balance budgets, figure out how to refinance a house, and even create a simple database. You don't have to be a bean counter to put Excel to good use.

As soon as you start Excel, a blank workbook awaits you. Each Excel file is a **workbook**. A workbook is simply a collection of **worksheets**, the sheets where you actually enter numbers and text. By default, Excel includes three sheets in every workbook. For many tasks, one sheet is all you need; but if you need more or less, you can easily add or subtract the sheets in a workbook.

Tasks

Task 1: Entering Data

Types of Data

Data you enter into a worksheet is contained in cells. You can enter text, numbers, dates, times, and formulas. Depending on the type of data, Excel will align the data differently inside the cell; text entries align to the left, number entries align to the right. As you type in the data, it appears in both the cell and the Formula Bar at the top of the worksheet.

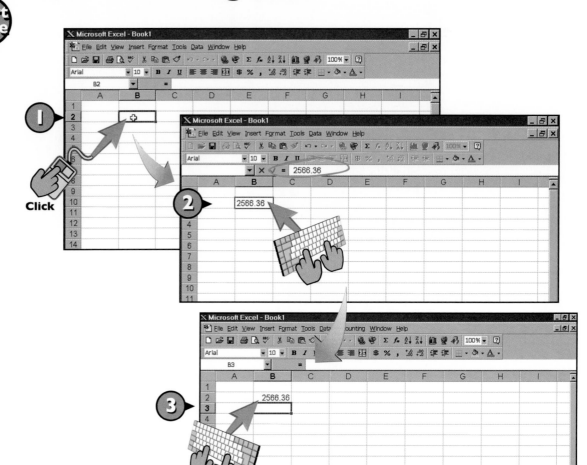

Start Here

Click

✅ Use the Number Pad

The strength of spreadsheet software is arithmetical calculations, so if you're planning to spend a lot of your time using Excel you should make an effort to get comfortable with the number pad on the keyboard.

1 ▶ Click inside the cell you want to use for data entry. A black border appears around the cell.

2 ▶ Type your data in the cell. The characters you enter are also placed in the Formula Bar.

3 ▶ Press **Enter** to move down one cell.

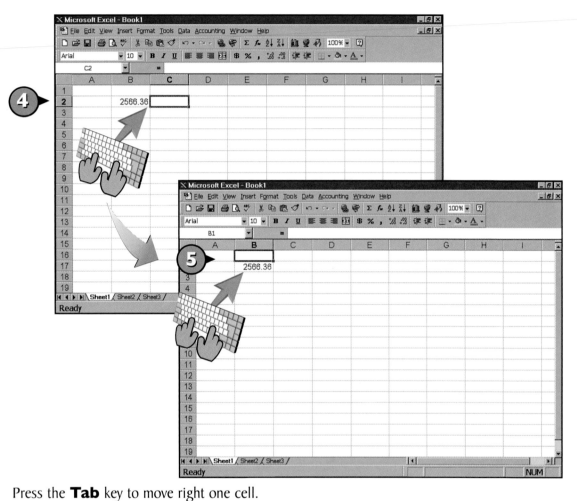

4 ▶ Press the **Tab** key to move right one cell.

5 ▶ Use the arrow keys to move in any direction.

✅ **Edit Entries**
If you make a mistake, it's usually faster to click inside the Formula Bar to edit the entry.

✅ **New Worksheet**
To open a new worksheet, click the **New** button on the toolbar. To open an existing worksheet, click the **Open** button and choose the file.

End Task

Task 2: Using AutoFill

Working with Data Series

Excel has a neat trick for speeding up data entry when the data is part of a series. The days of the week, the months, and numbers that have a specific interval are all series. Headings such as Qtr 1, Qtr 2, and Qtr 3 are also considered series data. With Excel's AutoFill feature, simply type in the first entry of the series and use the **Fill** handle to fill in the rest of the cells with the series.

✅ **Using a Number Series**

To create an automatic series of numbers, you must enter data in the first two cells, so Excel can figure out the interval.

✅ **Copying Data**

You can also use the Fill feature to copy the same data to adjoining cells. Type in the data in the first cell, select the cell, and use the **Fill** handle to copy the entry to adjoining cells.

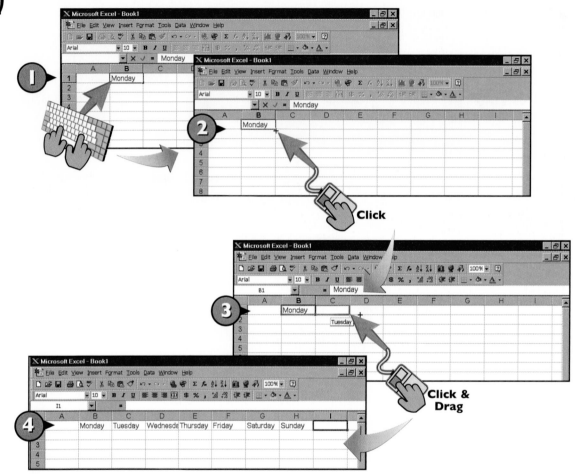

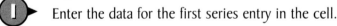

1▶ Enter the data for the first series entry in the cell.

2▶ Position your pointer at the lower-right corner of the cell. The pointer changes to a plus sign (+), called the **Fill** handle.

3▶ Press and hold the mouse button, and drag across the cells you want to use for the series (drag either right or down). As you pass each cell, a ScreenTip appears identifying the series content.

4▶ When you release the mouse, the series is filled in automatically.

Task 3: Deleting Cells

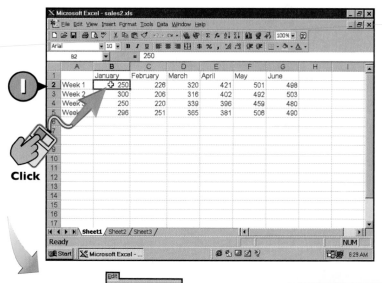

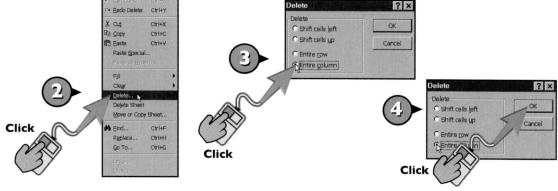

Using the Delete Command

If you have data that is no longer valid, it's quicker to delete the cells and enter new data than to delete and replace the data one cell at a time. Use Excel's Delete command to remove the entire cell or cells from the worksheet. When you delete cells, the adjacent row or column moves over to fill in the space.

Click

Click

Click

Click

1. Select a cell or drag to select multiple cells.

2. Open the **Edit** menu and choose **Delete**.

3. Delete the selected cells by specifying the way to shift adjacent cells. Or, delete the entire row(s) or column(s) in which the selected cell(s) reside.

4. Choose **OK**.

What About Formulas?
When rows or columns shift over, any formulas that reference those cells are updated to match the new settings.

Shortcut
You can also right-click on the cell and choose **Delete** from the shortcut menu.

Task 4: Clearing Cells

Removing Cell Contents Only

Clearing cells is the process of eliminating the contents of selected cells. This differs from deleting cells, because the cells themselves remain on the worksheet—only the contents are removed.

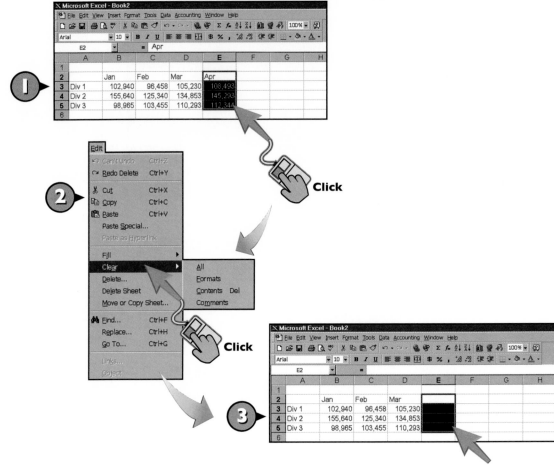

✓ **Clear Advice**
If you only need to replace the contents of one cell, it's easier to click on the cell and enter new data.

✓ **Selecting Multiple Cells**
Select multiple cells to clear by dragging across them. You can also select each cell by holding down the **Ctrl** key while you click.

✓ **Quick Clear**
Clear the selected cell or cells quickly by pressing the **Del** key.

1. ▶ Select the cell or cells you want to clear.

2. ▶ Choose **Edit**, **Clear**, and then choose a command from the submenu. You can clear the formatting, clear the contents, or clear any comments you've entered.

3. ▶ The cell contents are deleted as directed.

Task 5: Moving Data

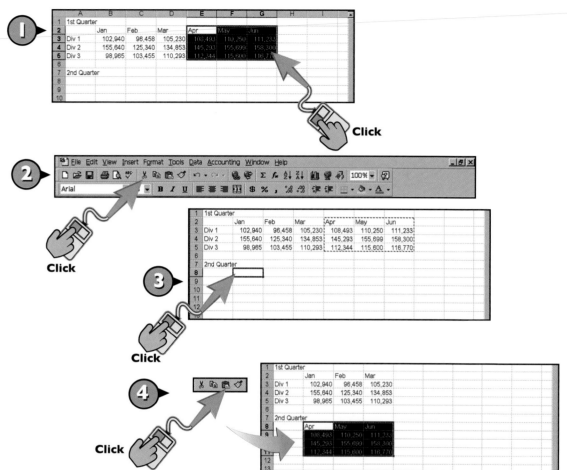

Click

Click

Click

Click

Using Cut and Paste

Sometimes you have to move data out of one part of your worksheet and put it in a new location. Use Excel's Cut and Paste commands to move data from one area of your worksheet to another, from one sheet to another, or from one workbook to another.

---

1 Select the cells you want to move.

2 Click the **Cut** button on the toolbar.

3 Move to the new location and select the first cell you want to move to.

4 Click the **Paste** button on the toolbar. The data is moved to the new location.

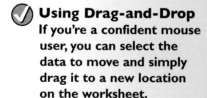

✓ **Using Drag-and-Drop**
If you're a confident mouse user, you can select the data to move and simply drag it to a new location on the worksheet.

✓ **Pasting Over Existing Cells**
If you paste the data into cells that already have existing data entered, the existing data is overwritten.

End Task

Task 6: Copying Data

Using Copy and Paste

When you copy data, the original data remains where it was and a copy of it is placed in a new location on the worksheet (or in a different worksheet). Use Excel's Copy and Paste commands to copy data into your current worksheet, another sheet, or even another workbook.

✓ **Copy Tip**
Copying a range of cells is handy if you need almost the same data in the new location. Copy everything, and then make the minor changes you need in the new location.

✓ **Using Drag-and-Drop**
If you're a confident mouse user, you can select the data to copy, hold down the **Ctrl** key and simply drag the data to another location on the worksheet.

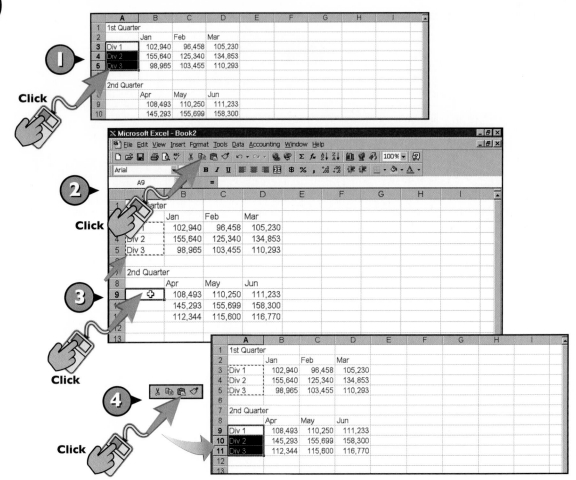

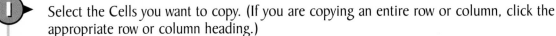

1 ▶ Select the Cells you want to copy. (If you are copying an entire row or column, click the appropriate row or column heading.)

2 ▶ Click the **Copy** button on the toolbar. (Notice a dash border now marks the selected data.)

3 ▶ Click the first cell in the new location you want to copy to.

4 ▶ Click the **Paste** button on the toolbar. The data is copied to the new location.

Task 7: Adjusting Column Width

Start Here

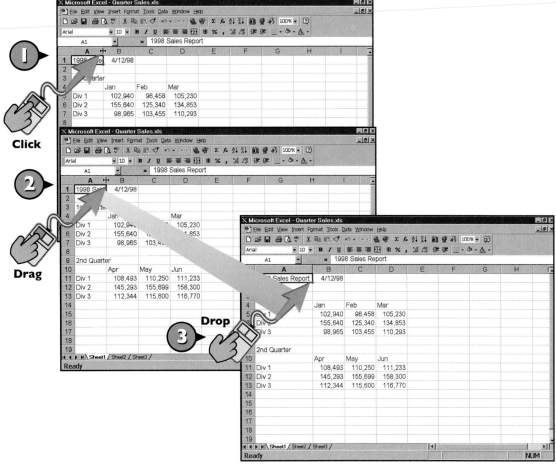

Click

Drag

Drop

Columns Not Wide Enough?

Sometimes the columns aren't wide enough to accommodate your data. When this happens, you may see truncated text, scientific notation (4.6E+09), pound signs (#####), or rounded decimals. Don't worry, none of your data is lost, it's just hidden. To see it all, you must widen the column.

✓ **Quick Fit**
Excel can quickly resize your column to the size of the widest entry. Just double-click on the border line to the right of the column heading.

✓ **Use the Column Width Box**
If you prefer to set a specific column width, select the column (or columns), choose **Format, Column, Width**. Set a new width and click **OK**.

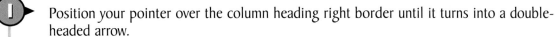

① Position your pointer over the column heading right border until it turns into a double-headed arrow.

② Drag to the right to widen the column. A vertical line travels with the pointer to show you where you are.

③ Release the mouse when the column width is correct and the column is resized.

Task 8: Formatting Numbers

Changing Number Formats

Use Excel's number formatting styles to change the way your numbers appear in the worksheet. The number's formatting style, such as currency or percent, will affect its meaning. Excel has a variety of number formats you can apply to make your number data meaningful.

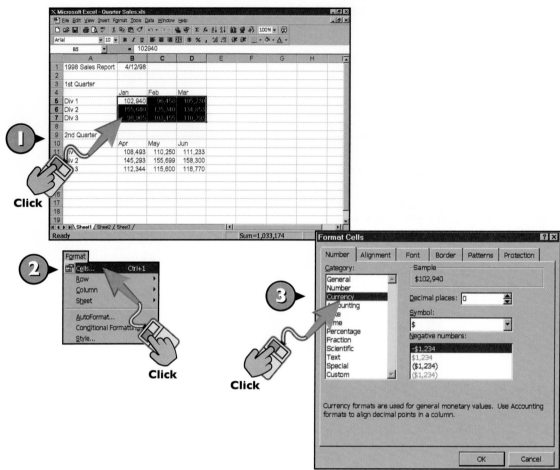

✓ **Plain Formatting**
By default, Excel assigns the General style format to numbers, which means the number entries appear as plain numbers—no frills.

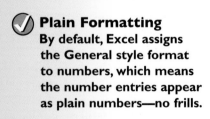

1. Select the cells you want to format (it's usually fastest to drag your mouse across them).

2. Open the **Format** menu and choose **Cells**.

3. In the Format Cells dialog box, choose the category that fits the numbers in the cells.

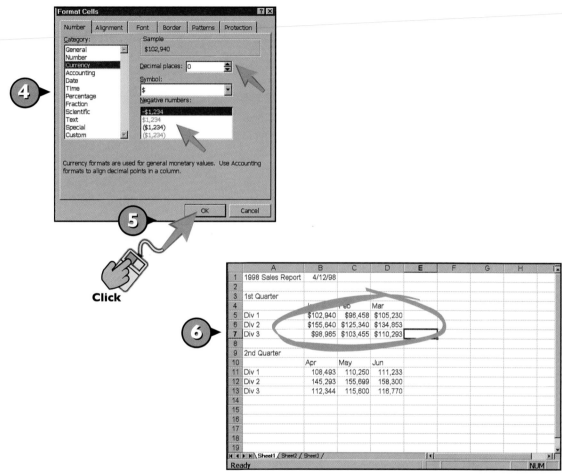

Click

 Specify the formatting style you want to use. Different categories have different choices.

 Click **OK**.

 The formatting style is applied to the number data.

 **Quick Formatting**
The three most commonly used number styles are available as buttons on the Formatting toolbar: **Currency** (adds dollar signs), **Percent** (adds percent signs), and **Comma** (adds commas). Just click the button you want to apply.

Task 9: Inserting a Column

Adding Columns

You can easily insert new columns in the middle of your data without having to worry about moving formula references. Using Excel's Insert command, you can add a column wherever you need it and all the data and formula references in the existing columns will adjust themselves.

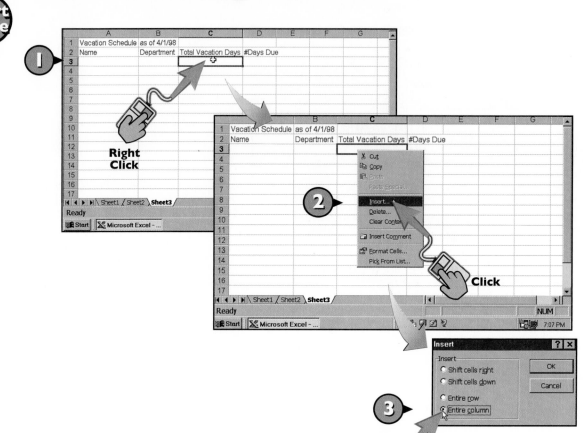

✓ Quick Column Select
You can also select an entire column by clicking the column header at the top of the column.

1 Right-click any cell in the column to the right of the place where you need to insert the new column.

2 Choose Insert from the shortcut menu.

3 In the Insert dialog box, select **Entire column**.

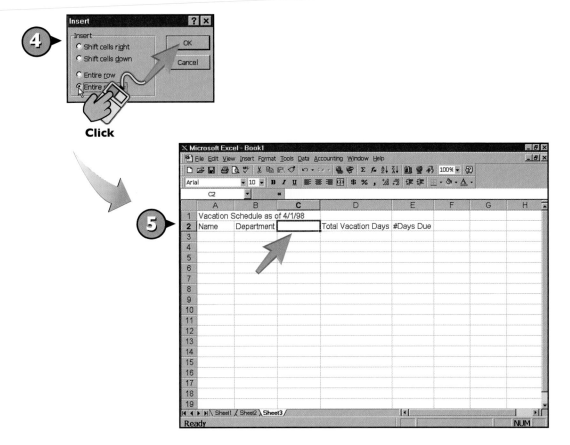

Click

4 Click **OK**.

5 The selected column moves to the right and a new column is inserted.

Task 10: Inserting a Row

Adding Rows

You can add rows to a worksheet with Excel's Insert command. Any existing data shifts to make room for the new rows and formula references are automatically updated. For example, I'm always inserting rows in worksheets because I frequently set up the first column in alphabetical order. It might be an employee list, an inventory list, or a shopping list. Then, of course, when a new item needs to be added to the list, it has to be put in its appropriate alphabetical place.

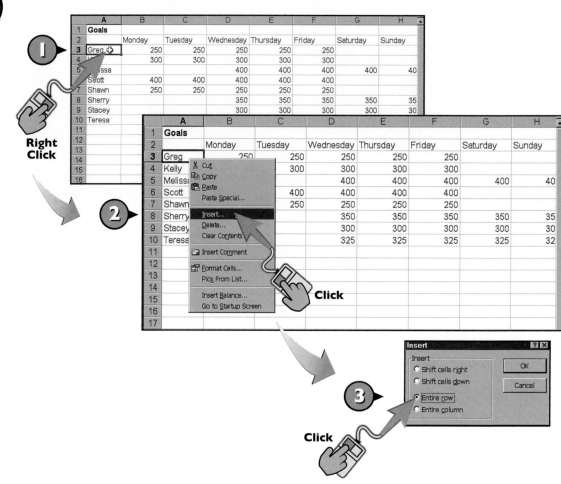

Start Here

Right Click

Click

Click

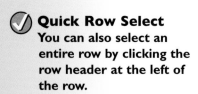

(✓) **Quick Row Select**
You can also select an entire row by clicking the row header at the left of the row.

1 ▸ Right-click any cell in the row below the place you need a new row.

2 ▸ Choose **Insert** from the shortcut menu.

3 ▸ In the Insert dialog box, choose **Entire row**.

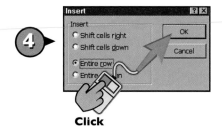

Click

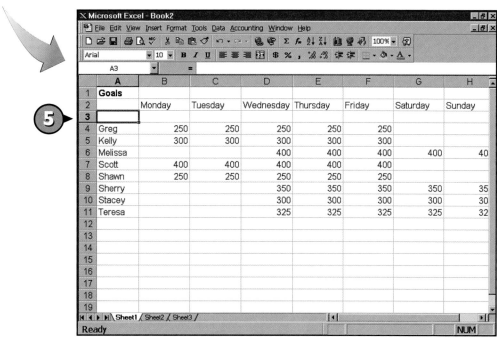

4 Click **OK**.

5 A new row is inserted into the worksheet.

Task 11: Entering a Formula Using Numbers

Using Mathematical Operators

Excel is essentially a calculator and you can create arithmetical formulas to take advantage of that fact. Formulas are sets of instructions for making a calculation. Excel uses mathematical operators, such as + (addition), – (subtraction), * (multiplication), and / (division) to perform calculations on numbers or cell contents. You can enter a formula directly into a cell, or use the Formula Bar.

✓ Operator Precedence

One rule to remember when creating formulas is *operator precedence*, which means Excel tackles a series of operations from left to right based on the operators involved. Excel always starts a calculation with any operations in parentheses, followed by exponential equations, multiplication and division, and finally addition and subtraction.

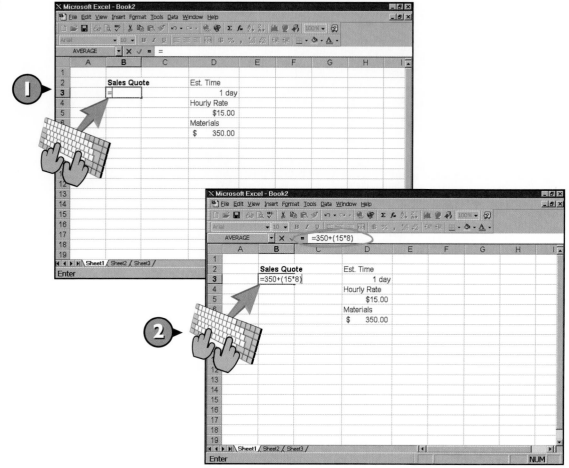

1 Click on the cell you want to use for the formula. Type an equal sign (=). This notifies Excel that you're about to enter a formula.

2 Enter the formula. You can use + (addition), – (subtraction), * (multiplication), and / (division). You can enclose subcalculations in parentheses. Press **Enter**.

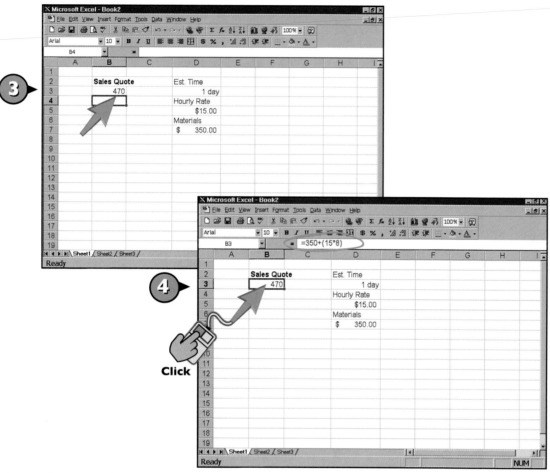

Click

3 The results are displayed in the cell.

4 Select the cell again to see the original formula in the Formula Bar.

 Always Use an Equal Sign
Another rule to remember regarding formulas is to always start your formulas with an equal sign. It's the law!

 Using the Formula Bar
Click inside the Formula Bar, click the equal sign, and start entering your formula. When finished, press **Enter** or click the green check mark button.

Task 12: Entering a Formula Using Cells

Using Cell References in a Formula

If you want to create a formula based on the information contained in cells, you don't have to type in the numbers; you can tell Excel to get the numbers from the cells. Each cell in a worksheet is identified by its cell address, or *reference*. A cell reference is its location in the worksheet based on column letter and row number. For example, the top left cell in the sheet is known as cell A1, the intersection of column A and row 1.

Click

✓ **Automatic Updates**
Using cell references means that the calculation is updated if any of the numbers in the cells change.

1 Select the cell in which you want to insert the formula. Type an equal sign (=) to notify Excel that you are entering a formula.

2 Click on the first cell to include in your formula and its address is inserted in the formula.

3 Enter the operator.

Spreadsheet 1 (Step 4)

Name box: AVERAGE | Formula Bar: =B5+C5

	A	B	C	D	E	F	G
1	1998 Sales Report	4/12/98					
2							
3	1st Quarter						
4		Jan	Feb	Mar	Totals		
5	Div 1	$102,940.00	$ 96,458.00	$105,230.00	=B5+C5		
6	Div 2	$155,640.00	125,340.00	$134,853.00			
7	Div 3	$ 98,965	$103,455.00	$110,293.00			
8							
9	2nd Quarter						
10		Apr	May	Jun			
11	Div 1	108,493.00	$110,250.00	$111,233.00			
12	Div 2	$145,293.00	$155,699.00	$158,300.00			
13	Div 3	$112,344.00	$115,600.00	$116,770.00			

Click

Spreadsheet 2 (Step 5)

Name box: E6 | Formula Bar: =

	A	B	C	D	E	F	G
1	1998 Sales Report	4/12/98					
2							
3	1st Quarter						
4		Jan	Feb	Mar	Totals		
5	Div 1	$102,940.00	$ 96,458.00	$105,230.00	$ 304,628.00		
6	Div 2	$155,640.00	$125,340.00	$134,853.00			
7	Div 3	$ 98,965.00	$103,455.00	$110,293.00			
8							
9	2nd Quarter						
10		Apr	May	Jun			
11	Div 1	$108,493.00	$110,250.00	$111,233.00			
12	Div 2	$145,293.00	$155,699.00	$158,300.00			
13	Div 3	$112,344.00	$115,600.00	$116,770.00			

Spreadsheet 3 (Step 6)

Name box: E5 | Formula Bar: =B5+C5+D5

	A	B	C	D	E	F	G
1	1998 Sales Report	4/12/98					
2							
3	1st Quarter						
4		Jan	Feb	Mar	Totals		
5	Div 1	$102,940.00	$ 96,458.00	$105,230.00	$ 304,628.00		
6	Div 2	$155,640.00	$125,340.00	$134,853.00			
7	Div 3	$ 98,965.00	$103,455.00	$110,293.00			
8							
9	2nd Quarter						
10		Apr	May				
11	Div 1	$108,493.00	$110,2	,233.00			
12	Div 2	$145,293.00	$155	58,300.00			
13	Div 3	$112,344.00	$115,	$116,770.00			

Click

(4) Click the next cell to enter its address in the formula. Repeat the process to add more cells to the formula.

(5) Press **Enter** to put the results in the cell.

(6) Select the cell to see the formula in the Formula Bar.

Edit Formulas
To make any changes to a formula, select the cell containing the formula, and make your corrections on the Formula Bar.

Task 13: Using AutoSum

Start Here

Summing Up Cells

When you need to add the total for a contiguous (adjoining) group of cells, use the Excel AutoSum feature. It's one of the handiest tools in Excel. You can quickly sum up numbers with a click of a button.

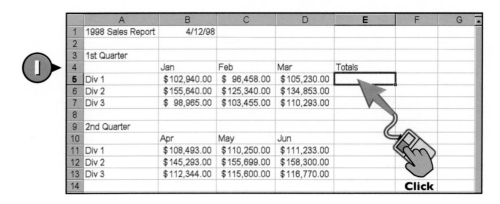

Click

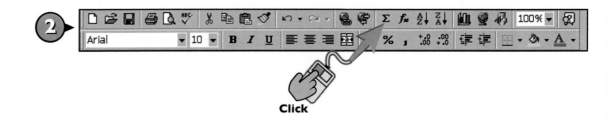

Click

 **Quick Totals**

To sum a group of numbers without entering the total in a cell, check out the Sum option on the status bar. Select the cells you want to total and look at the **SUM** option on the status bar for a quick summary.

 Click in an empty cell at the end of a contiguous group of cells (you can also work with either a row or column).

 Click the **AutoSum** button on the toolbar.

Next Step

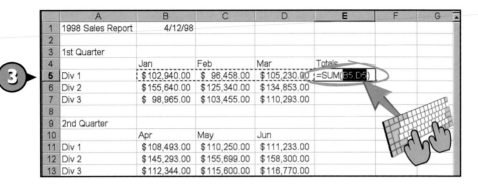

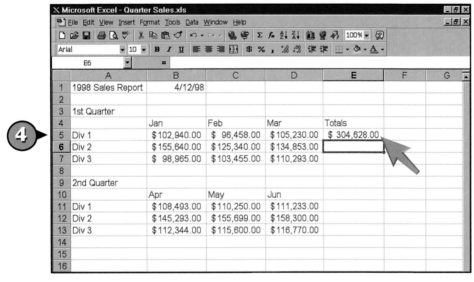

3 ▶ AutoSum enters the sum formula that includes the adjoining cells. Notice the cells AutoSum selects to total are surrounded by a dash border. Press **Enter**.

4 ▶ AutoSum sums the cells.

✓ **Wrong Cells?**
If AutoSum grabs the wrong cells to total, you can drag another set of cells to sum.

Task 14: Calculating an Average

Using the Average Function

Use Excel's Average function to help you quickly average values in your worksheet. The Average function is just one of Excel's many functions—complex ready-made formulas that perform a series of operations on a specified range of values, such as averaging numbers.

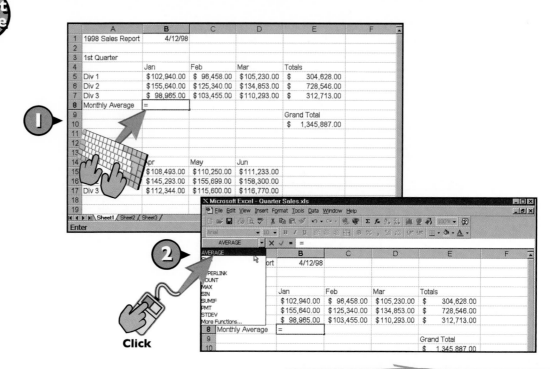

✓ **What's a Range?**
A group of related cells is called a *range*. Ranges form a block of cells and you can select them and apply formulas or functions to the entire group of values.

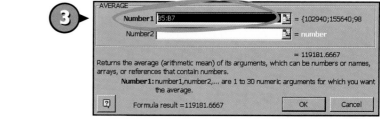

✓ **Wrong Cells?**
If the function grabs the wrong cells to average, click inside the Function dialog box and enter the correct cells, and then click **OK**.

1️⃣ Select the cell in which you want to place the average (choose an empty cell next to the set of numbers you want to average). Enter an equal sign to indicate a formula.

2️⃣ Click the drop-down arrow to the right of the Function box and choose **Average** from the list of functions.

3️⃣ Excel assumes the range you want to average is the range of cells either above or to the left of the cell. Check the cell references for accuracy.

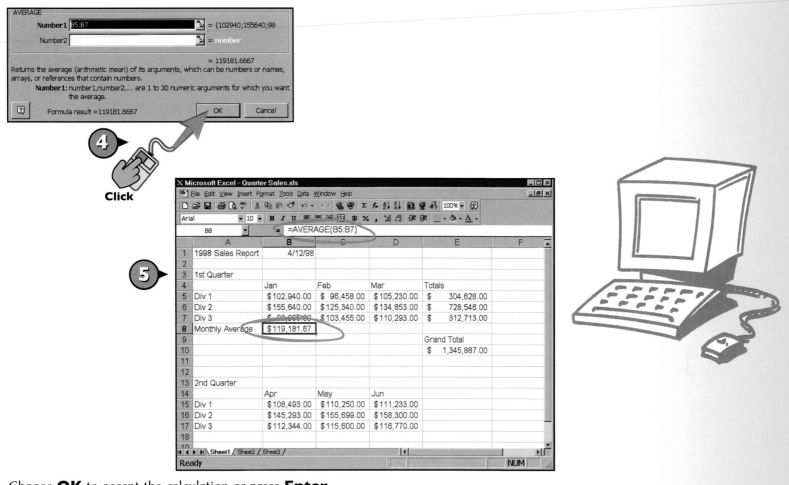

Click

AVERAGE
Number1 B5:B7 = {102940;155640;98
Number2 = number

= 119181.6667
Returns the average (arithmetic mean) of its arguments, which can be numbers or names, arrays, or references that contain numbers.

Number1: number1,number2,... are 1 to 30 numeric arguments for which you want the average.

Formula result =119181.6667 OK Cancel

X Microsoft Excel - Quarter Sales.xls

File Edit View Insert Format Tools Data Window Help

Arial ▼ 10 ▼ B I U

B8 = =AVERAGE(B5:B7)

	A	B	C	D	E	F
1	1998 Sales Report	4/12/98				
2						
3	1st Quarter					
4		Jan	Feb	Mar	Totals	
5	Div 1	$102,940.00	$ 96,458.00	$105,230.00	$ 304,628.00	
6	Div 2	$155,640.00	$125,340.00	$134,853.00	$ 728,546.00	
7	Div 3	$ 99,285.00	$103,455.00	$110,293.00	$ 312,713.00	
8	Monthly Average	$119,181.67				
9					Grand Total	
10					$ 1,345,887.00	
11						
12						
13	2nd Quarter					
14		Apr	May	Jun		
15	Div 1	$108,493.00	$110,250.00	$111,233.00		
16	Div 2	$145,293.00	$155,699.00	$158,300.00		
17	Div 3	$112,344.00	$115,600.00	$116,770.00		
18						

Sheet1 / Sheet2 / Sheet3 /

Ready NUM

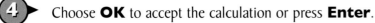

④ Choose **OK** to accept the calculation or press **Enter**.

⑤ Excel averages the values and displays the results.

End Task

Task 15: Getting a Count

Using the Count Function

Excel's Count function can quickly tally the number of items in a range of cells, particularly if the worksheet is really long and you don't want to waste time scrolling and counting the entries yourself. For example, if you create a long product list, use the Count function to tally how many products are on back order in the worksheet.

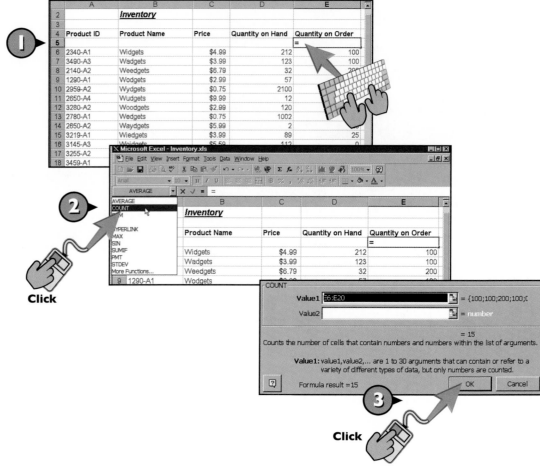

Click

Click

✓ Can't See the Cells?
If the Function dialog box is in your way of viewing a range, click the **Collapse** button at the end of the Value text box and the Function box is reduced to a bar. Click the button on the bar to reopen the box.

1 Select the cell in which you want to place a count (usually a cell next to the range). Enter an equal sign (=).

2 Click the **Function** drop-down arrow next and choose **Count** from the list of functions.

3 Excel assumes you're counting the adjacent cells. If that assumption is correct, press **OK** to put the count in your selected cell.

Next Step

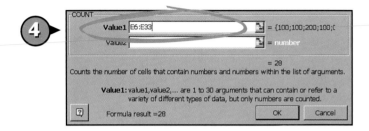

④ COUNT

Value1 E6:E33 = {100;100;200;100;0

Value2 = number

= 28

Counts the number of cells that contain numbers and numbers within the list of arguments.

Value1: value1,value2,... are 1 to 30 arguments that can contain or refer to a variety of different types of data, but only numbers are counted.

Formula result =28

OK   Cancel

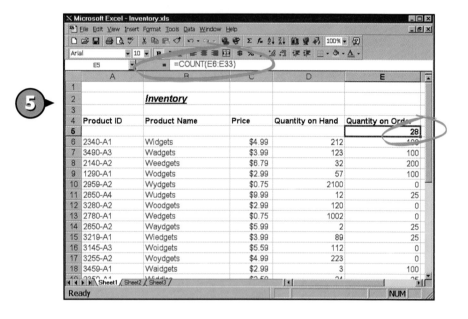

⑤

X Microsoft Excel - Inventory.xls

File Edit View Insert Format Tools Data Window Help

Arial   10

E5   =   =COUNT(E6:E33)

	A	B	C	D	E
1					
2		Inventory			
3					
4	Product ID	Product Name	Price	Quantity on Hand	Quantity on Orde
5					28
6	2340-A1	Widgets	$4.99	212	100
7	3490-A3	Wadgets	$3.99	123	100
8	2140-A2	Weedgets	$6.79	32	200
9	1290-A1	Wodgets	$2.99	57	100
10	2959-A2	Wydgets	$0.75	2100	0
11	2650-A4	Wudgets	$9.99	12	25
12	3280-A2	Woodgets	$2.99	120	0
13	2780-A1	Wedgets	$0.75	1002	0
14	2650-A2	Waydgets	$5.99	2	25
15	3219-A1	Wiedgets	$3.99	89	25
16	3145-A3	Woidgets	$5.59	112	0
17	3255-A2	Woydgets	$4.99	223	0
18	3459-A1	Waidgets	$2.99	3	100

Sheet1 Sheet2 Sheet3

Ready   NUM

④ If you want to count a different range of cells, click inside the **Value1** box and enter the correct cell range.

⑤ Excel counts the items in the range and displays the results.

Need Help?
Click the **Help** button in the Function dialog box for accessing the **Office Assistant** and finding help for working with the Function dialog box.

End Task

Task 16: Using a Named Range in a Formula

Inserting Range Names

After you've created named ranges, it's much easier to use the range contents in formulas. For example, it's quick and easy to enter **Qtr1** in a formula instead of **B3:B30.** You can insert range names into formulas you create using the Formula Bar, or into formulas you create using the Function dialog box.

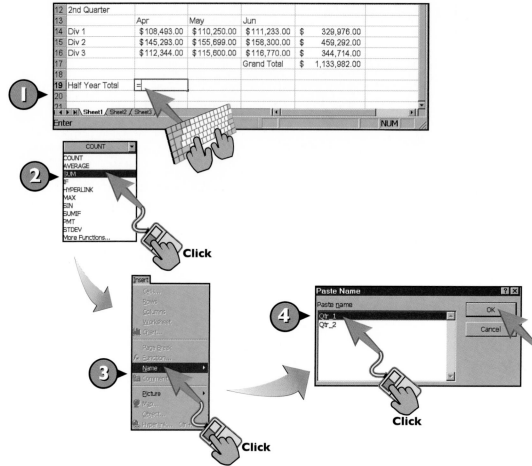

✓ Deleting Range Names

To delete range names, open the **Insert** menu, select **Name,** and then **Define.** Select the range name and click **Delete.** Click **OK** to exit.

1 ▶ Select the cell you want to use for the formula and enter an equal sign (=).

2 ▶ Click the **Function** drop-down arrow and choose a function from the list.

3 ▶ When the Function dialog box opens, instead of entering cells choose **Insert, Name, Paste** to open the Paste Name dialog box.

4 ▶ Select the named range you need and choose **OK.**

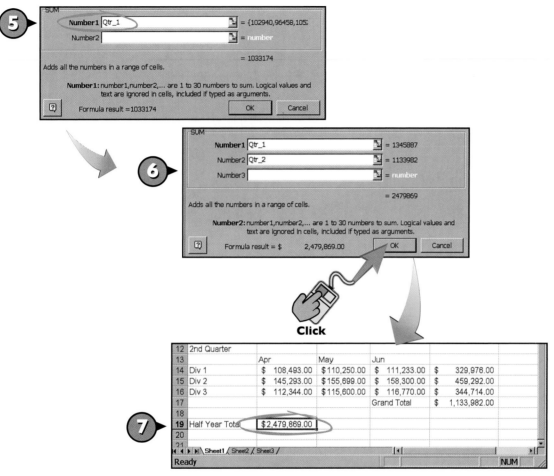

Click

5▶ The range name is inserted in the Function dialog box.

6▶ Continue entering range names for the formula as needed. Choose **OK** when finished.

7▶ The formula results appear in the cell.

Task 17: Naming a Range of Cells

Working with Ranges

A group of related cells is called a *range*. Ranges form a block of cells and are named by their anchor points, the upper-left cell and the lower-right cell in the block, such as **A1:D5** (a colon separates the references). But the range name **A1:D5** doesn't tell you much about its contents. To make your ranges more meaningful, you can assign names, such as **QTR1** or **SALES**. You can then use the range name in a formula and know exactly what data it's referring to.

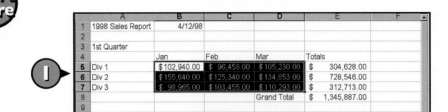

Start Here

Click

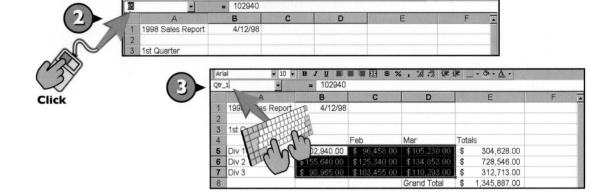

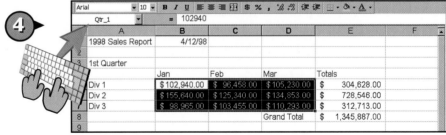

✓ **Range Rules**

Always start a range name with a letter or underscore. You can use as many as 255 characters in a range name, but no spaces are allowed (use an underscore or period in place of a space).

1 ▶ Select the range of cells you want to name.

2 ▶ Click in the **Name** box. Excel presents the location of the first cell as a name. The name is highlighted, so the first character you type will replace the existing characters.

3 ▶ Type in a name for the range (remember, no spaces allowed).

4 ▶ Press **Enter**, and the name is assigned.

End Task

Task 18: Sorting Data

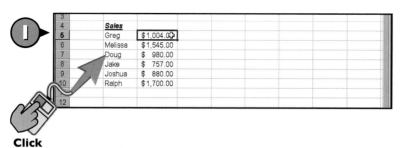

Click

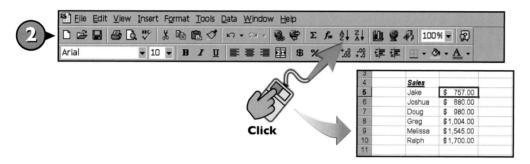

Click

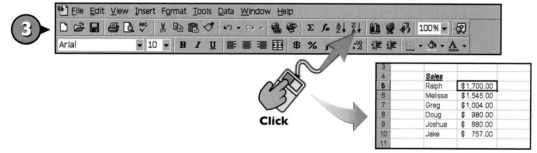

Click

Using Sort Commands

Use Excel's Sort commands to get different views of your worksheet data. For example, you may want to view the highest sales figures at the top of your worksheet. Use a descending sort to display the sales numbers from highest to lowest.

✓ **Alphabetized?**
Depending on the type of data you select to sort, a sort may be numerical in order or alphabetical.

❗ **Undo!**
Be sure to click the **Undo** button on the toolbar immediately after sorting. Sorting scrambles your data, and unless you wanted it sorted permanently, use the **Undo** button before saving the file.

---

① To sort a column quickly, click any cell in the column (or click the column header).

② To sort the column from lowest to highest, click the **Sort Ascending** button on the toolbar.

③ To sort the column from highest to lowest, click the **Sort Descending** button.

Task 19: Finding Data

Searching Through Your Worksheet Data

When worksheets get extremely large, it can be difficult and time consuming to search for exactly the data you need to view or work on. Use Excel's Find command to help you locate data.

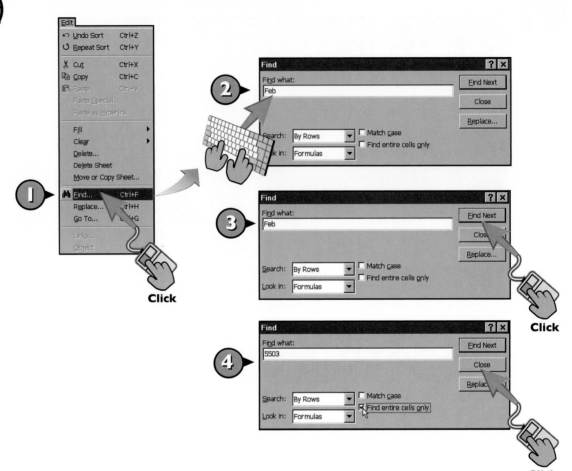

Click

Click

Click

✓ **Need an Exact Match?**
Select the **Find entire cells only** check box in the Find dialog box to locate the cell with the exact match. For example, use this option to avoid cells that contain 567 and 5699 when searching for 56.

✓ **Go To**
If you're working on an extremely large worksheet, use the Go To command to quickly move to a cell. Press **Ctrl+G**, type the cell reference and press **Enter**.

1 ▶ Open the **Edit** menu and select **Find**.

2 ▶ Enter the data you want to search for in the **Find what** text box.

3 ▶ Click **Find Next** to see the first match.

4 ▶ If that's the cell you need, choose **Close** or choose **Find Next** again until you get to the right place.

End Task

Task 20: Hiding Data

Start Here

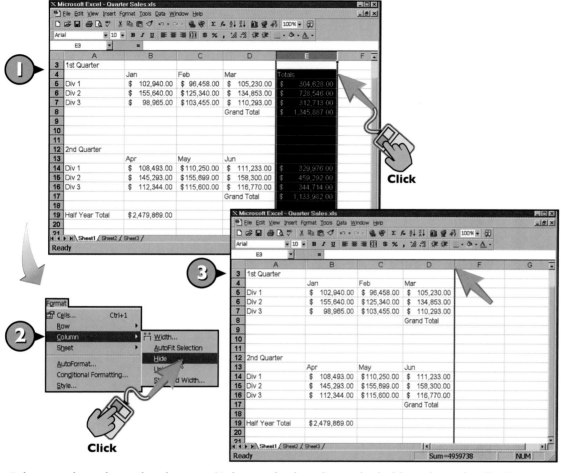

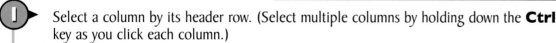

Click

Click

Using the Hide Command

Hiding a row or column of data isn't just a way to keep the information from prying eyes. It also makes it easier to work in a large worksheet. The hidden columns and rows close up, making navigation a bit faster.

✓ **Need to Hide Rows?**
This exercise hides a column, but if you want to hide a row, just apply the same logic and steps, using rows.

✓ **Unhiding Columns**
To unhide a column, press **Ctrl+G** to display the Go To dialog box. Enter X1 in the Reference box (where X is the hidden column number) and choose **OK**. A black line now appears where the hidden column sits. Choose **Format, Column, Unhide**.

1 ▶ Select a column by its header row. (Select multiple columns by holding down the **Ctrl** key as you click each column.)

2 ▶ Open the **Format** menu and select **Column**, **Hide**.

3 ▶ The column is now hidden from view.

End Task

Task 21: Saving a Worksheet

Using the Save Command

You should save your worksheet right after you start working in it, and then continue to save often. That way, if something happens to the power, or your computer freezes, you'll only lose the data you entered after the last time you saved.

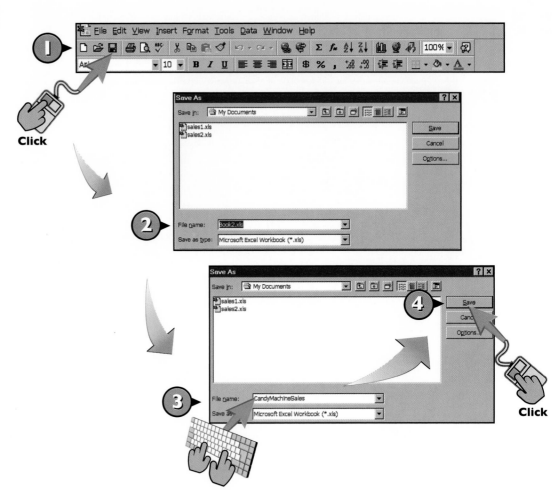

Click

Click

✓ **Saving Existing Files**
To save a previously saved worksheet that already has a name, click the **Save** button on the Standard toolbar. The file is saved without revisiting the Save As dialog box.

✓ **Renaming Sheets**
You can easily rename the individual sheets within an Excel workbook file. Right-click on the **Sheet** tab, select **Rename**, and type in a new name. Press **Enter**, and you're done.

1 ▶ Click the **Save** button on the Standard toolbar.

2 ▶ The first time you save a worksheet, the Save As dialog box appears. Excel suggests a name, and it's highlighted so as soon as you enter a character all the original characters disappear.

3 ▶ Enter an appropriate name in the **File name** text box (you don't have to type **.xls**, it's added automatically).

4 ▶ Click **Save**.

End Task

Task 22: Opening a Worksheet

Start Here

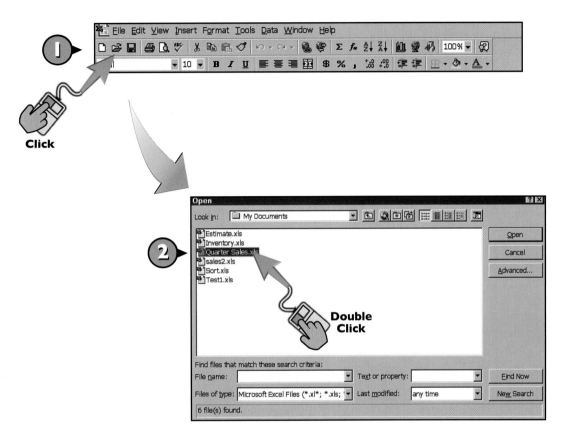

Click

Double Click

After you've saved a worksheet, you'll probably want to open it again at another time to work on it some more. Use Excel's Open command to quickly summon any worksheet you've previously saved.

 Which Workbook?
If there are many worksheets to choose from in the Open dialog box, you can change the view and see more information about the files by clicking the **Details** button. The Details view shows the size and last saved date of the file.

 Opening New Sheets
When you open an Excel workbook, there are three worksheets ready to use: **Sheet1, Sheet2,** and **Sheet3.** Click a **Sheet** tab at the bottom of the window to switch between them. To add a sheet, select **Insert, Worksheet.** To delete a sheet, make it active and select **Edit, Delete Sheet** and click **OK** in the confirm box.

Click the **Open** button on the Standard toolbar.

In the Open dialog box, locate the worksheet you want to use. Double-click the worksheet name and it immediately opens in the Excel window.

Task 23: Using Save As

Creating Duplicate Files Under New Names

You can save another copy of a worksheet under a different name. This is useful if you want to make a backup copy, or to save a worksheet with certain calculations and then make changes to the calculations. If things don't work, you still have the original saved copy.

✓ Saving as Other File Formats

If you want to give a file to someone who has an earlier version of Excel, or a different spreadsheet program, click the **Save as type** drop-down arrow, choose the appropriate file type, and then choose **Save**.

❗ What About the Save Button?

You can't access the Save dialog box by clicking the **Save** button on the Standard toolbar. To save the file under a new name, choose **File, Save As**.

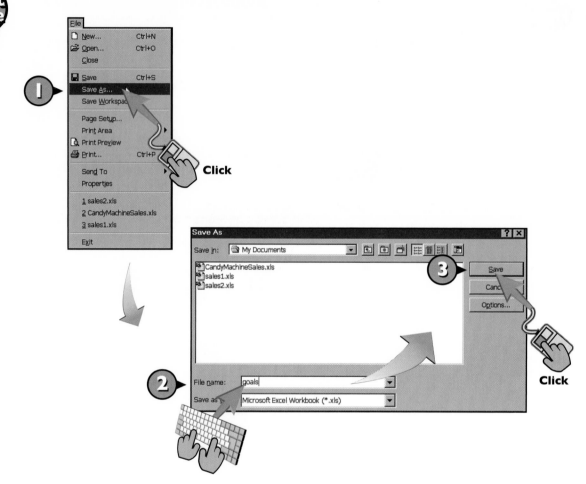

Open the **File** menu and select **Save As**.

The Save As dialog box appears with the current filename already entered. Enter a new filename.

Click **Save**.

Task 24: Printing

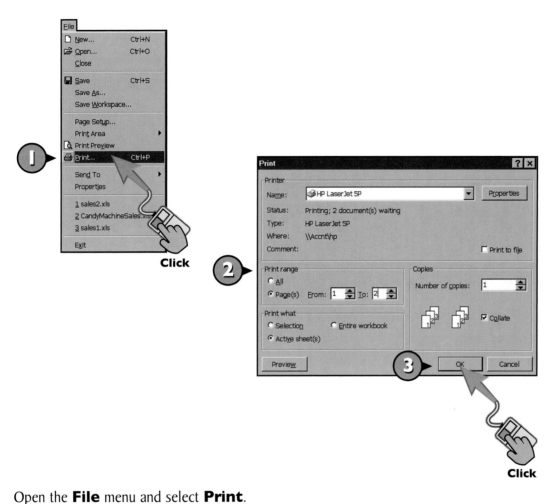

Click

Click

Using the Print Command

Eventually you'll want to make a hard copy of your worksheet (that's jargon for printed copy). Use Excel's Print command to print out the current sheet, a selected range, or the entire workbook.

① Open the **File** menu and select **Print**.

② Make any adjustments needed to the print options: You can change printers, print multiple copies, specific pages, or a range that you selected before opening the dialog box.

③ Click **OK**, and your data is printed.

Quick Print
To print the entire worksheet, using the default printer and settings, click the **Print** button on the Standard toolbar.

PART 3

Outlook

Microsoft Outlook is a powerful tool for managing your time, email, contacts, and daily tasks. Outlook is a collection of features you can use to stay organized. It's almost like having your own personal secretary in a box. You can use Outlook to schedule appointments and maintain your calendar, build a database of business contacts and their address and email information, keep track of important tasks, jot down electronic notes to yourself, and even manage your email needs, including composing and sending email messages.

When you open Outlook, a collection of tools appears as a list of folders on the left side of the screen. They include Inbox, Calendar, Contacts, Tasks, Journal, and Notes. The toolbar at the top of the program window gives you quick access to commands associated with each tool. To open a tool, click its icon in the list. By default, Outlook starts you out with the Inbox displayed so that you can read new email messages.

In this part of the book, you learn how to utilize Outlook's many features. For example, learn how to compose an email message, attach a file to the message, and send it to a recipient found in your electronic address book.

Tasks

Task 1: Opening an Outlook Folder

Using Outlook's Folders

Each Outlook component is organized into folders. The folders, in turn, are organized into three groups: Outlook (contains all the main features, such as Calendar and Tasks), Mail (contains folders for managing your mail), and Other (for working with other computer files and folders on your system). The easiest way to navigate Outlook's folders is with the Outlook Bar, the vertical bar at the left of the program window containing icons that represent Outlook's components.

✓ The Folder List

Another way to display Outlook's components is with the Folder List. Click the **Folder List** button on the toolbar, then click the **Folder** you want to display. The **Folder List** button toggles on or off to display or hide the Folder List.

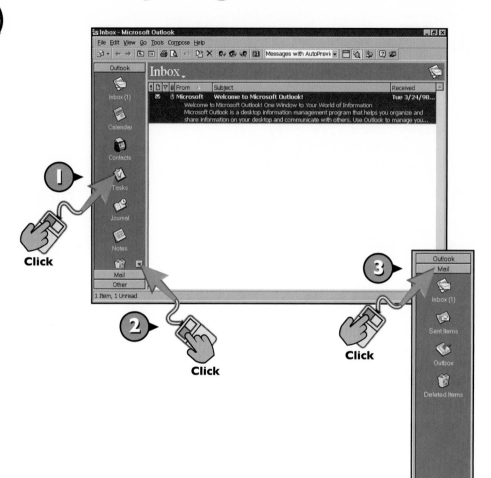

1 ▶ Click any icon in the Outlook Bar to open that folder. For example, click **Tasks** to display the Tasks folder.

2 ▶ Use the Outlook Bar's scroll arrow to display different icons on the bar.

3 ▶ To change folder groups, click on the appropriate Group button. For example, to open the Mail group, click the **Mail** button.

Task 2: Viewing the Inbox

Start Here

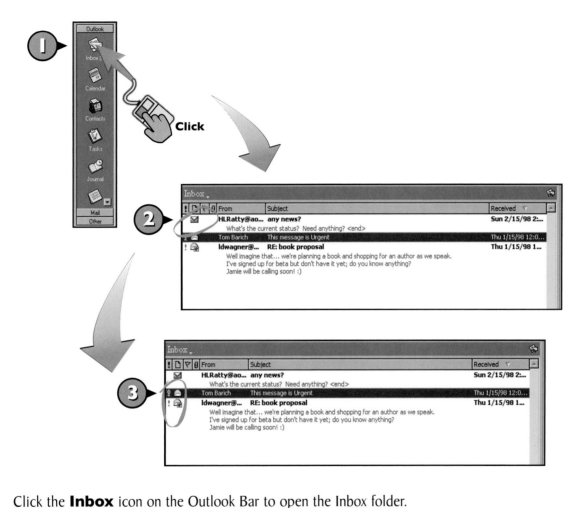

Click

Using the Inbox

The Inbox collects your mail and displays information about the mail you've received, such as who sent the mail, when it was received, its priority level, the subject matter, and more.

---

1 ▶ Click the **Inbox** icon on the Outlook Bar to open the Inbox folder.

2 ▶ Unread messages have closed envelopes icons and show the first three lines of the message so you can decide which message you want to read first.

3 ▶ The columns next to the messages contain special icons, including read and unread envelope icons. For example, an exclamation point indicates an urgent message.

✅ **How Many Messages?**
The Inbox icon on the Outlook Bar also indicates how many new messages are waiting for you to read.

End Task

Task 3: Viewing the Personal Address Book

What's the Address Book?

Outlook provides a personal address book you can use to store email addresses for the people you correspond with. Whenever you compose a new email message, you can access the address book to select a specific address to use.

✓ Using Network Mail?

If you're connected to a network mail system, you also have a network address book, in addition to your personal address book, that contains email addresses of everyone on your network.

✓ Adding Entries

Learn how to add entries to your address book in Part 3, Task 4, "Adding an Entry to Your Address Book." Learn how to compose email messages in Part 3, Tasks 5, "Opening an Email Message Form," and 6, "Addressing an Email Message."

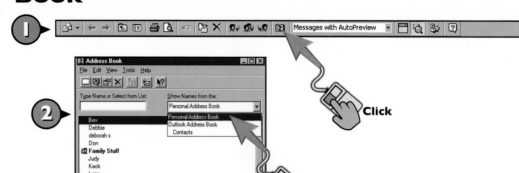

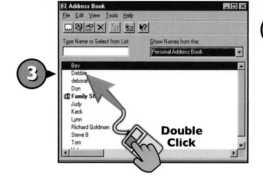

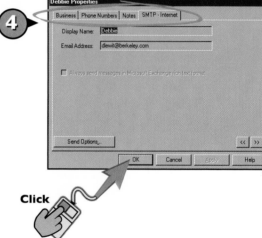

1 Click the **Address Book** button on the toolbar to open your Address Book.

2 Click the **Show Names from the** drop-down arrow and select **Personal Address Book** to display your address list.

3 Double-click an entry to see more information about the entry in the Properties dialog box.

4 You can use the tabs to view additional information about this person. Click **OK** to return to the Address Book.

Task 4: Adding an Entry to Your Address Book

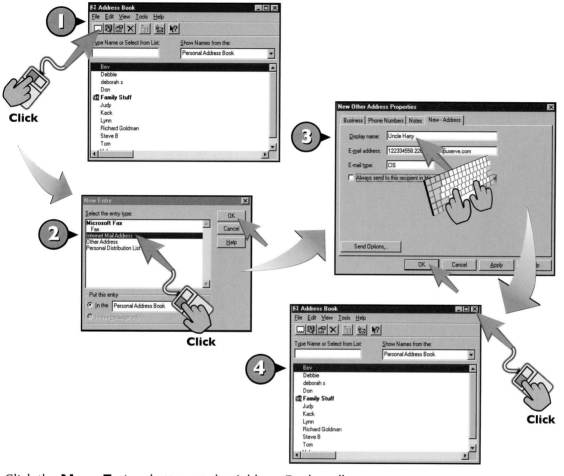

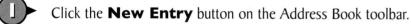

Click

Click

Click

Adding Address Entries

You can have different types of entries in your address book, depending on the services you installed for Outlook. For example, if you use Outlook for faxing, you can keep fax recipients in your address book. Outlook makes it easy to add new entries to your book with the New Entry command.

✓ Open the Address Book

Remember: To open the Address Book dialog box, click on the **Address Book** button on the toolbar while viewing the Inbox folder.

✓ Adding Details

The other tabs in the Properties dialog box give you options for keeping important data about an entry. For example, you can add business phone numbers, fax numbers, and notes pertaining to the person.

1 ▶ Click the **New Entry** button on the Address Book toolbar.

2 ▶ Choose the type of entry such as **Internet Mail Address**, and so on, and then click **OK**.

3 ▶ Enter a **Display Name** the way you want it to appear in your address book and an email address. Click **OK** to save your entry and return to the Address Book dialog box.

4 ▶ You can repeat these steps to add more entries, or click the **Close** button to exit the Address Book dialog box.

Task 5: Opening an Email Message Form

Understanding the Message Form

When you're ready to send an email message, Outlook provides a message form you can fill in. It includes text boxes for entering addresses and subject matter and a toolbar with formatting options you can use to make your message text more attractive. (Learn how to fill in the form and send the message in the tasks to follow.)

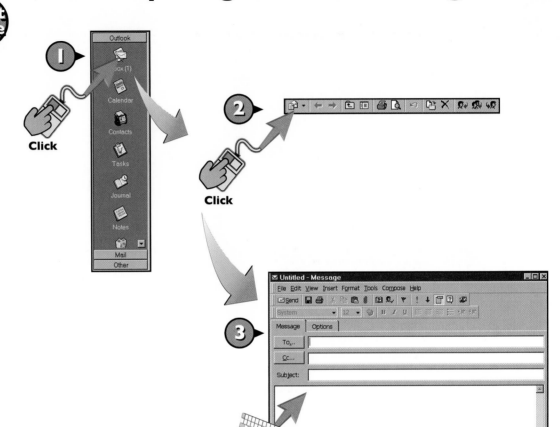

Start Here

Click

Click

✅ Opening Forms from Other Folders

If you're working in another folder in Outlook, choose **File, New, Mail Message** from the menu bar (or you can press **Ctrl+Shift+M**) to quickly open a message form.

 Select **Inbox** from the Outlook Bar.

 Click the **New Mail Message** button on the toolbar.

 When the message form opens, you can compose your note.

 End Task

Task 6: Addressing an Email Message

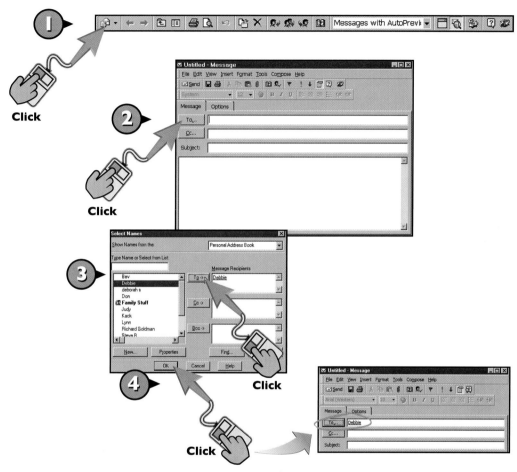

Click

Click

Click

Click

Click

Inserting an Address

The most important part of a message is the address of the recipient. Use Outlook's Personal Address Book to quickly insert email addresses you've stored in your address book.

✓ **Typing in the Address**
If your recipient isn't in your address book, you can enter an email address directly into the message form. Simply click in the **To** text box and type in the address.

❗ **WARNING**
When addressing your email, if you type one misplaced comma or one incorrect letter, the message won't get there. Make sure you've entered the address correctly.

✓ **Where's My Address Book?**
If your Personal Address Book isn't listed in the Select Names dialog box, use the **Show Names from the** drop-down arrow to select an address book.

 From the Inbox folder, open a message form by clicking on the **New Mail Message** button on the toolbar.

 Click the **To** button to open the Select Names dialog box which lists your personal address book.

 Select the recipient from the left list box, then click **To**, which places the name in the Message Recipients box. Repeat the process if you're sending the message to multiple recipients.

 Click **OK** when you've finished selecting recipients. The recipient's name now appears on the message form.

End Task

Task 7: Sending Copies of a Message

Using the Cc Option

Use the message form's carbon copy field (Cc...) to send a copy of your message to other recipients to keep them informed about the correspondence or to keep them posted on what's going on in a particular project. Like the To field described in the previous task, you can tap into your personal address book to insert Cc recipient's email addresses.

✅ **Typing In Addresses**
If the recipient isn't listed in your address book, you can enter an email address directly into the **Cc** field. Simply click in the text box and type in the address.

✅ **Fill in the To Field!**
When filling in a message form you're going to carbon copy to someone else, be sure to enter the primary recipient's address in the **To** field first. See Part 3, Task 6 to learn how.

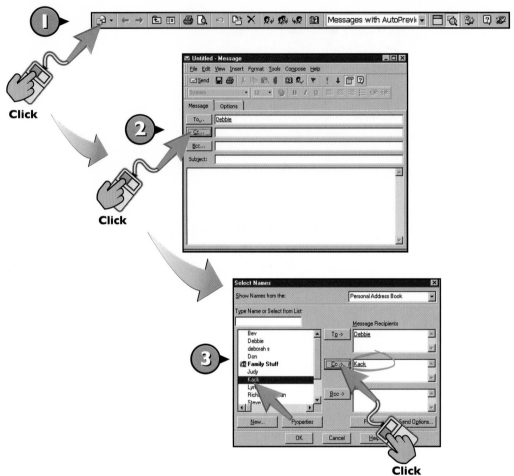

1 From the Inbox folder, click on the **New Mail Message** toolbar button to open a message form.

2 Click the **Cc** button on the message form to open the Select Names dialog box listing your address book.

3 Select the recipient from the left list box, then click **Cc**, which places the name in the appropriate Message Recipients box.

Next Step

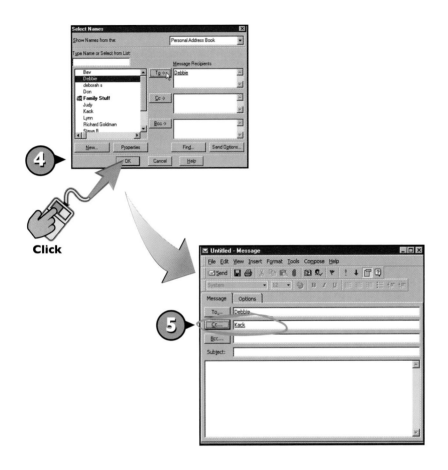

Click

 Repeat for any additional recipients to whom you want to send copies. When you are finished, choose **OK**.

 The names you selected appear in your email form's Cc field.

 Where's My Address Book?
If your Personal Address Book isn't listed in the Select Names dialog box, use the **Show Names from the** drop-down arrow to choose the address book you want to use.

Task 8: Composing Your Message Text

Using the Subject Box and Message Box

After you address your message, you need to enter a subject matter title and the message text itself. The subject matter gives your recipient an idea of the text of the message, which can be important to someone who receives numerous email messages and has to set priorities for reading them.

✅ **Formatting Cautions**
Keep in mind that any formatting you add to a message may not necessarily be seen by the recipient, particularly if the recipient doesn't use Outlook.

✅ **Viewing ScreenTips**
To find out what any message form toolbar button does, hover your mouse pointer over a button to view the ScreenTip.

Start Here

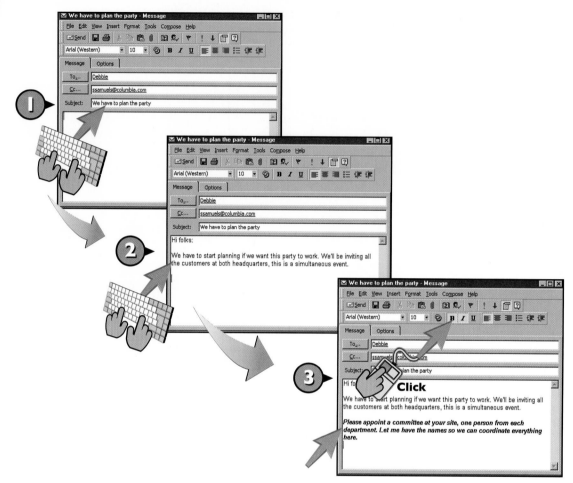

1 In an open email message form, click anywhere in the **Subject** box and enter a short phrase describing your message. The title bar of your message form now displays your subject.

2 Click inside the text box and enter the text of your message.

3 Use the formatting tools on the message form's toolbar to enhance your text—for example, to bold or italicize a word. Select the text and click the appropriate button.

Task 9: Sending a Message

Start Here

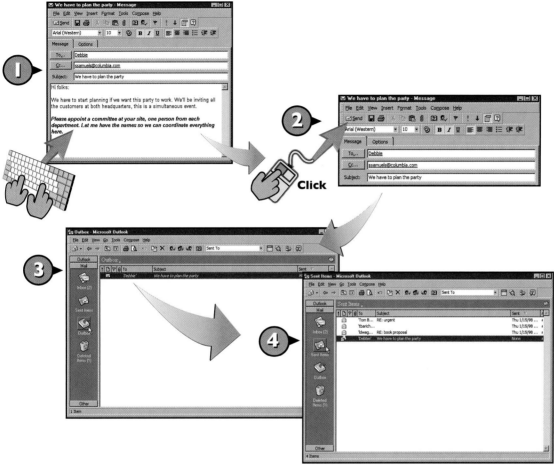

Click

1

Address and compose your email message.

2 Click the **Send** button on the Message Form toolbar.

3 The message form disappears—it has moved to the Outbox where it waits for you to connect to your mailbox. Log on to your Internet connection, and your message is sent.

4 After it's sent to a mail server, the message travels to your Sent Items folder. If you don't need a copy of it, delete it from the folder to save disk space.

Using the Send Command

After you've composed a message, you're ready to send it electronically. When you send email with Outlook, all Internet email messages go to the Outbox where they wait for you to log on to your Internet connection before sending. If you're on a network, your messages are sent as soon as you click the Send button.

✓ On a Network?
If you're on a network email system, the message only stays in the Outbox for a nanosecond before going to the server.

✓ Deleting Messages
To delete a sent message from the Sent Items folder, select the message and press **Delete**. The message is removed to the Deleted Items folder. Don't forget to clean out your Deleted Items folder before exiting Outlook (open the **Tools** menu and select **Empty "Deleted Items" Folder**).

End Task

Task 10: Attaching a File to a Message

Attaching Files

You can easily send files, called *attachments*, from other applications along with your email messages. For example, you may want to send a colleague the latest report you've compiled in Word, or perhaps you need to send someone a copy of your Outlook task list. You can use Outlook's Insert File command to attach the file to an email message.

✓ **Software Compatibility**
Your recipient must have the software you used to prepare the file to open and read your attachment.

✓ **Free Viewers!**
Your Microsoft Office Small Business Edition CD has a Word viewer and an Excel viewer you can lend to others who don't have the software necessary to view your Word or Excel file attachments. Check out the Office ValuPack for more information.

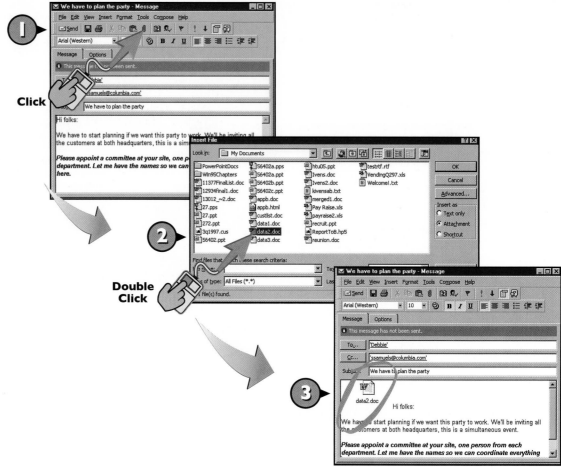

Start Here

Click

Double Click

1 ▶ From your prepared message, click the **Insert File** button on the Message Form toolbar.

2 ▶ The Insert File dialog box opens. Locate the file you want to attach. Double-click the file to attach it to your message.

3 ▶ An icon appears in your message to indicate that a file is attached.

End Task

Task 11: Opening Mail

Start Here

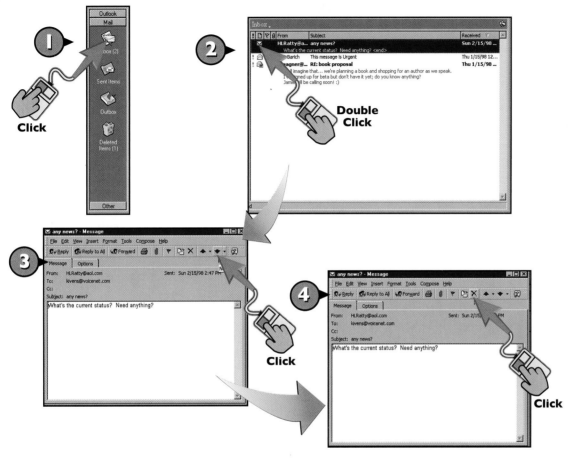

Click

Double Click

Reading Messages

Open your email messages in Outlook's Inbox folder. When mail arrives in your Inbox, you will want to read it and perhaps respond to it. You can decide which mail is more important (or interesting) by looking at the subject lines or paying attention to icons that indicate urgency.

✔ Closing Messages
To quickly close an email message, click the Close button (×) located in the upper-right corner of the form. The message is marked as read (with an open envelope icon) and remains in the Inbox until you move or delete it.

✔ Deleting Messages
Deleted messages are placed in Outlook's Deleted Items folder. Don't forget to empty the folder before exiting Outlook (select **Tools, Empty "Deleted Items" Folder**).

1. Click the **Inbox** icon on the Outlook Bar.

2. Double-click the message you want to open.

3. Read the message. To open the next message, click the **Next Item** button on the message form's toolbar.

4. If you don't need to save the message, delete it by clicking the **Delete** button on the toolbar.

End Task

Task 12: Replying to Mail

Responding to Messages

Outlook makes it easy to reply to the email messages you receive and open. A simple click on the Reply button is all it takes to open up another message form in which you can type a reply.

✓ **Replying to Everyone**
If the original message had additional recipients in the Cc field, click **Reply to All**, and your reply message will be mailed to each recipient.

✓ **Forwarding Messages**
Use the message form's **Forward** button to send the message to someone else. You must then fill in the address of the person to whom you want to forward the message.

✓ **What About the Original Message?**
When filling out the reply message form, you can leave the original message intact, or you can delete it (select the message text and press **Delete**).

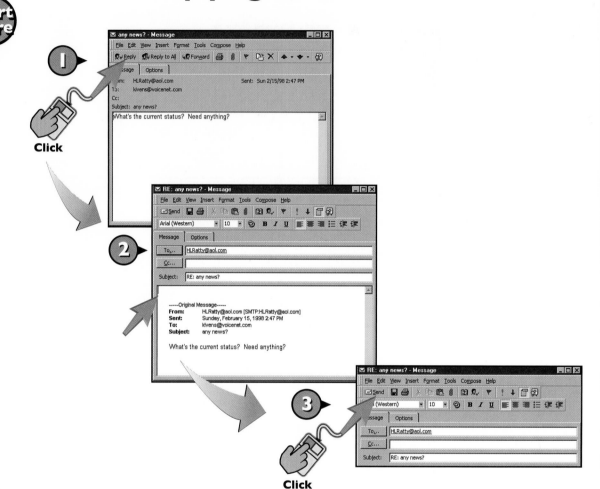

Click

Click

1 ▶ Open the message to which you want to reply. Click the **Reply** button on the Message toolbar.

2 ▶ A message form opens with the recipient and subject fields already filled in. The original message is in the text box and your insertion point is waiting for you to enter your reply message.

3 ▶ After you enter the text of your message, choose **Send**.

End Task

Task 13: Editing Your Reply

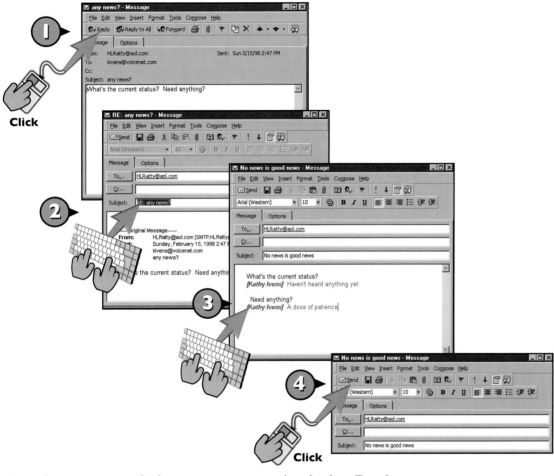

Click

Click

Creating a Reply Message

By default, when you reply to a message the original subject title remains, with **RE:** in front of it to indicate a response. You can choose to leave the original subject title, or replace it with a new one. The original message text is also displayed in the message box. You can leave the original message intact, or you can delete it. You can also select specific parts of the original message to respond to and rearrange the text as necessary in your response.

1. Open the message to which you want to respond and select **Reply**.

2. To change the subject text, if needed, select the text and type in a new subject title.

3. Delete any text in the message box that isn't necessary, leaving the sentences to which you are responding, and type in your own reply text.

4. Click the **Send** button to dispatch the reply.

✓ **Distinguishing Replies**
As you respond to individual lines in a message reply form, Outlook inserts your name so that the recipient can distinguish your typing. Outlook also uses another font color for your reply text.

End Task

Task 14: Forwarding Mail

Using the Forward Option

When you get email that you think someone else might be interested in, or enjoy, you can forward it using Outlook's Forward command.

✅ Using the Address Book

You can use addresses you've stored in your personal address book when you forward messages. Simply click the **To** button and choose a recipient from your address list. (See Part 3, Task 3, "Viewing the Personal Address Book," for details on using the address book.)

✅ Adding Notes

Before forwarding the message, you can add a new note in the message box or edit the original message text, if needed.

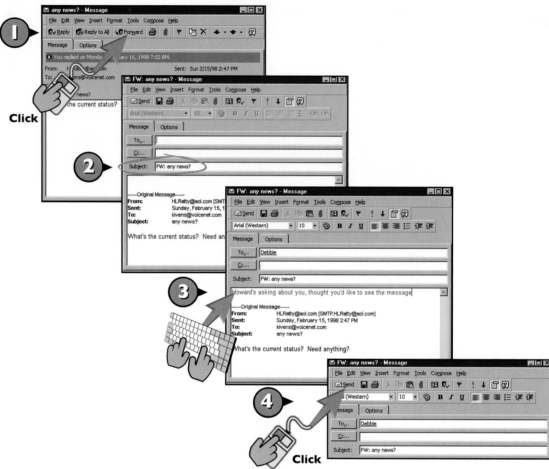

Click

Click

1. ▶ With your message open, click the **Forward** button on the Message toolbar.

2. ▶ A new message form opens with the subject box filled in (with **FW:** in front of the text to indicate the message is being forwarded). The original message is in the message box.

3. ▶ Enter the recipient's email address in the **To** field.

4. ▶ Click the **Send** button.

Task 15: Opening Attachments You Receive

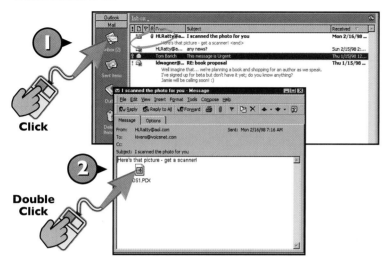

Click

Double Click

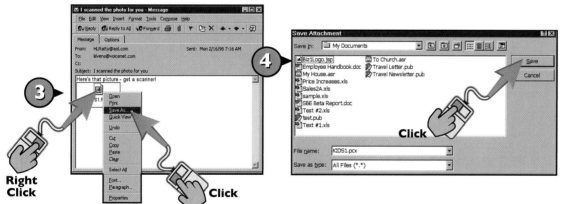

Right Click

Click

Click

Working with File Attachments

When you receive a message with an attached file, you can easily open the attachment from within Outlook. However, you must have either the same software used to create the file or a viewer program that lets you convert the file into something you can read.

✅ **Saving Attachments**
It's a good idea to save your attachment file in another folder so you won't have to open the message to find it again. This is especially true if you plan to delete the message.

✅ **Free Viewers!**
The Office 97 Small Business Edition CD comes with several viewer programs in the ValuPack that you can use or share with others for viewing Word, Excel, or PowerPoint files if these applications are not installed on the computer.

---

1 ▶ To view your message list, click the **Inbox** icon on the Outlook Bar. If a message has an attachment, you'll notice a paper clip icon in the Attachment column.

2 ▶ When you open the message, the attachment is represented by an icon in the message text. Double-click the icon to open the associated software and view the file.

3 ▶ To save the file, right-click on the **attachment** icon and choose **Save As** from the shortcut menu.

4 ▶ Choose a folder in which to save the file, then click **Save**.

Task 16: Viewing the Contacts Folder

Viewing Contacts

Use Outlook's Contacts folder to keep track of the people you contact the most, including addresses, phone numbers, and personal information such as birthdays and anniversaries.

(✓) **Using Address Card View**

When using Address Card view, you can click the alphabet tabs at the far right of the window to look through your list alphabetically. This is particularly helpful when you have a large list of contacts.

Click

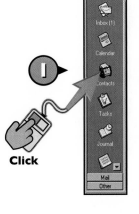

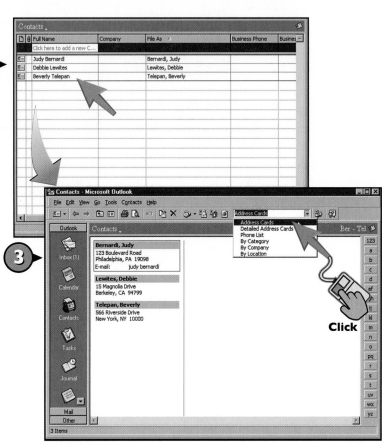

Click

① ▶ Click the **Contacts** icon on the Outlook Bar.

② ▶ When the Contacts folder opens, all the contacts you've created are listed.

③ ▶ Click the **Current View** drop-down arrow and select a new view to change how the contacts are displayed.

End Task

Task 17: Creating a New Contact

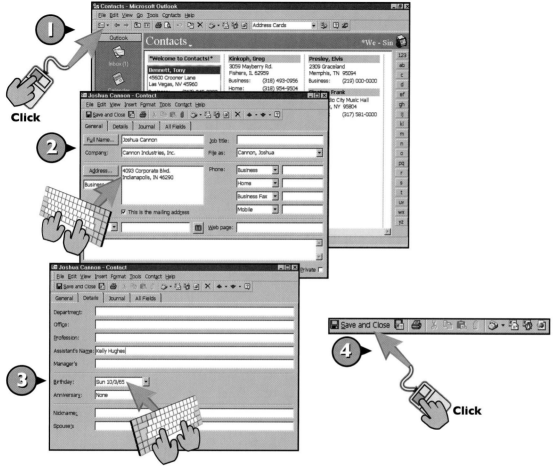

Click

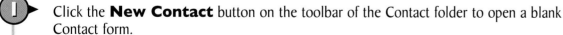

Click

Adding New Contacts to the Folder

You can easily add contacts, such as business clients or family members, to your Contacts folder list using a Contact form. You'll find fields for entering the person's name, address, phone numbers, email address, and more.

✓ Turning Email into Contacts

When you receive email, you can add the sender to your contact list. Right-click on the sender's name in the message and choose **Add to Contacts**. A new Contact form opens with the sender's name and email address already filled in. Enter any additional information, then click **Save** and **Close**.

✓ Continue Adding Contacts

To keep adding contacts, click the **Save** and **New** button on the Contact Form toolbar. This saves your current contact information and opens another form to fill in.

---

1 ▶ Click the **New Contact** button on the toolbar of the Contact folder to open a blank Contact form.

2 ▶ In the General tab, click inside the **Full Name** text box and enter the contact's name. Fill in each field as necessary. Use the **Tab** key to move from field to field.

3 ▶ Use the Details tab to add more information about the contact, such as a birthday or anniversary.

4 ▶ Click the **Save and Close** button to save the contact and add it to the contacts list.

Task 18: Editing a Contact

Changing Contact Information

You can quickly add changes to any contact in your list, such as updating phone numbers or addresses. You can even delete old contacts you no longer need.

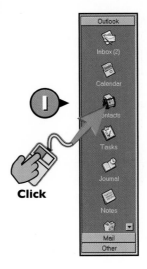

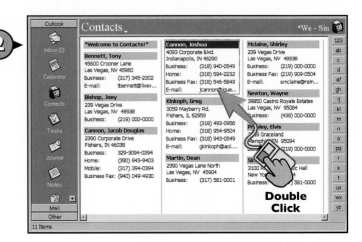

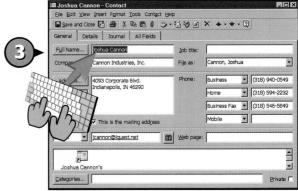

✓ Adding Details

Use the Details tab to add information about your contact such as birthdays, spouse's name, and other personal details.

1 Click the **Contacts** button to open the Contacts folder.

2 Double-click on the contact you want to change. This opens the Contact form.

3 Make any changes to the fields and tabs as needed in the Contact form.

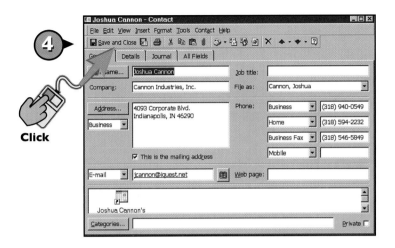

Click

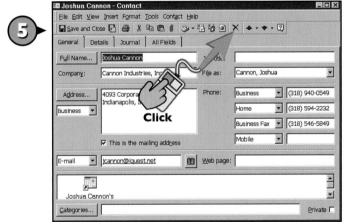

Click

④ Choose **Save and Close** when you're finished making changes.

⑤ To remove a contact from your list, select the contact from the list and press **Delete**.

✓ **Deleting Contacts**
Any contacts you delete from the Contacts list are placed in Outlook's Deleted Items folder. Don't forget to delete items from the folder before exiting Outlook. Open the **Tools** menu and select **Empty "Deleted Items" Folder.**

End Task

Task 19: Sending Email to Contacts

Creating a Message from a Contact

Sending email to a contact is easy, and you don't even have to move to the Inbox to use the **New Message** icon. You can accomplish the task right from the Contacts folder.

Start Here

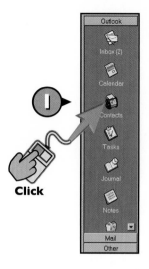

Click

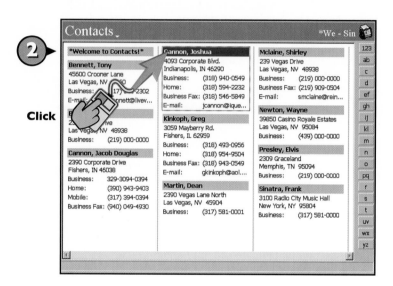

Click

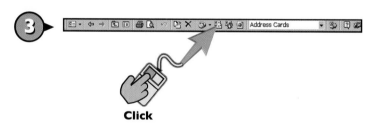

Click

✓ **Enter an Address**
Before you can email a contact, you need to make sure you've entered the contact's email address in the email address field of the Contact form.

Click the **Contacts** icon on the Outlook Bar to open the Contacts list.

Select the contact you want to send email to.

Click the **New Message to Contact** button on the Outlook toolbar.

Next Step

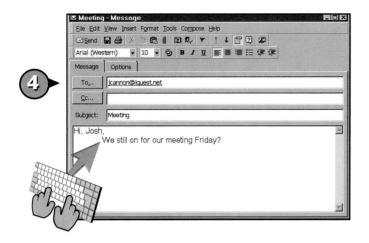

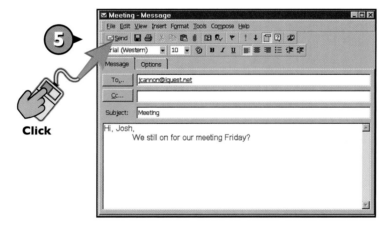

4 The Message form opens with the contact's address added as the recipient. Enter your email subject and text.

5 Click **Send**.

Task 20: Creating a Task

Using the Task Folder

Outlook's Task folder can help you organize things you need to do. You can record each task you need to accomplish, such as a to-do list or a project check-list, or even a list of groceries you need to pick up on the way home. After creating a task list, you can then check off the items as you complete them.

✓ **Use Simple List View**
The easiest way to add a task is to use the Simple List view in your Task folder. To switch to this view, click the **Current View** drop-down arrow on the toolbar and select **Simple List**.

✓ **Seeing Tasks in Calendar**
Outlook's task list is also displayed in the Calendar folder in miniaturized form so you can see what tasks you need to accomplish for each day.

Start Here

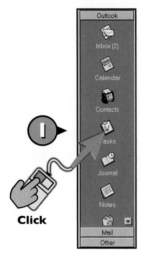

Click

Click

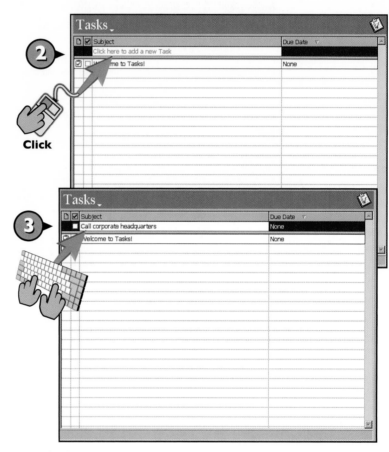

1 ▸ Click the **Tasks** icon on the Outlook Bar.

2 ▸ Click on the top line of the list where it says **Click here to add a new Task**.

3 ▸ Enter a description of the task.

Next Step

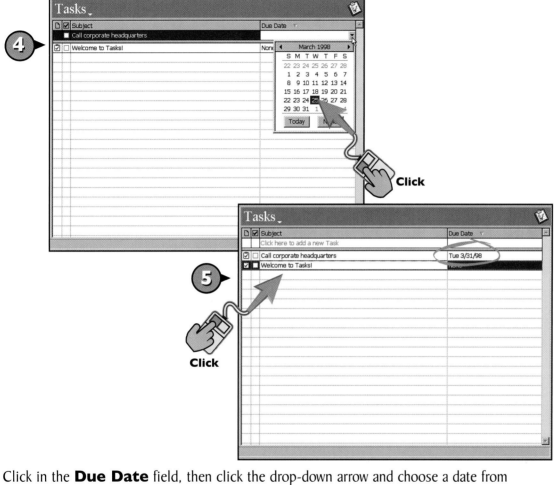

Click

Click

4 ▶ Click in the **Due Date** field, then click the drop-down arrow and choose a date from the calendar.

5 ▶ Click anywhere in the Task folder to save the task and add it to your list.

✅ **Entering Due Dates**
You can type a date directly into the **Due Date** field of a task. Just click in place and type in a date.

End Task

Task 21: Tracking Task Dates and Status

Tracking Tasks

Some tasks have a due date, and some tasks have multiple due dates as the various parts of the task are completed. You can keep track of dates and the task's status if your task items require this level of attention. Outlook's Task form has several options for tracking a task's progress.

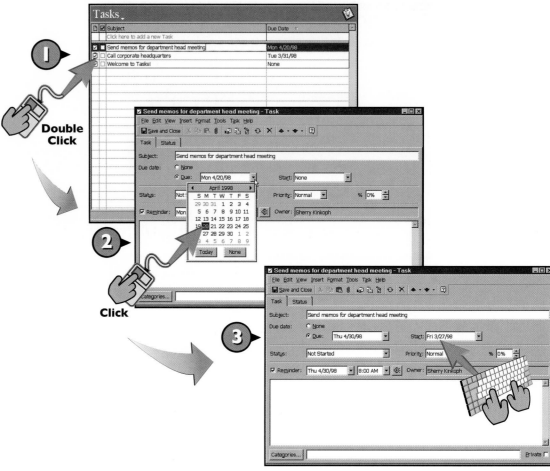

Start Here!

Double Click

Click

✅ Editing Tasks

You can edit or add to a task's details at any time by opening its Task form (double-click the task from the Task list). Make any changes and click Save and Close.

1 ▶ From the Task list folder, double-click the task you want to track or edit.

2 ▶ To change the task's due date, click the **Due** drop-down arrow and choose a new date.

3 ▶ Optionally, you can fill in a **Start** date to mark the beginning of the task.

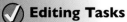

Next Step

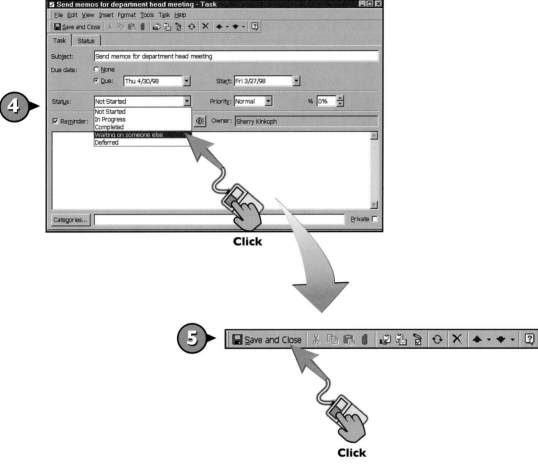

Click

Click

4 ▶ Click the **Status** drop-down arrow to select a status assignment.

5 ▶ Choose **Save and Close** to save your changes.

Task 22: Creating Reminders for Tasks

Assigning Reminder Alarms

You can assign a reminder alarm to a task to help you remember it. When the specified date or time occurs, Outlook's Reminder prompt appears to let you know about the task.

Outlook Must Be Running

For Outlook's reminder feature to remind you about a task, you must have Outlook running. You don't have to have the program window displayed—you can minimize it by clicking the **Minimize** button in the upper-right corner of the program window. This reduces the Outlook window to a button on your Windows 95 taskbar. This way, Outlook can run in the background while you work with other applications and you won't miss any reminders.

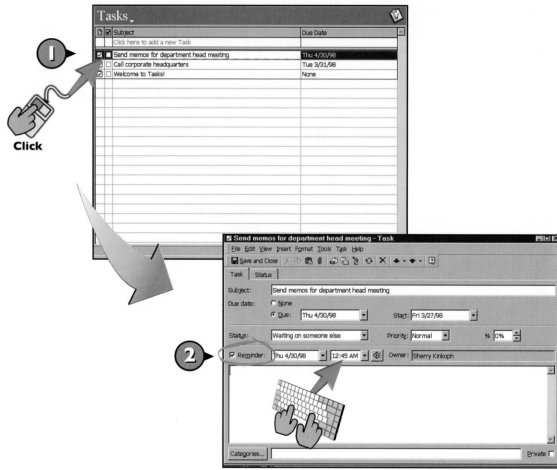

Click

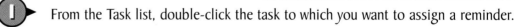

1 From the Task list, double-click the task to which you want to assign a reminder.

2 Select the Reminder check box and enter the date and time you want to be prompted about the task.

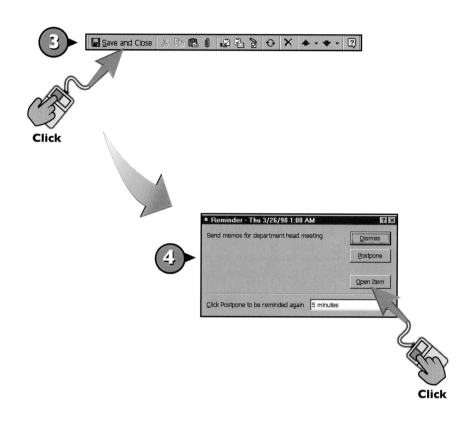

Click

Click

③► Click **Save and Close**.

④► When the specified date and time occurs, a reminder prompt appears. Click **Open Item** to open the Task form.

Changing Alarm Sounds
When you select the reminder option, a default audio sound is assigned as well. If you prefer to use another sound file as a reminder, click the speaker icon in the Task form to open the Reminder Sound dialog box. Click the **Browse** button and locate another .WAV file that you would like to use.

Dealing with the Reminder Prompt
When the Reminder prompt appears, click **Postpone** to delay the reminder for another five minutes. You can use the drop-down list at the bottom of the prompt box to set a new reminder time. To close the Reminder prompt, click **Dismiss**.

Task 23: Creating an Appointment with Calendar

Scheduling Appointments

Use Outlook's Calendar folder to keep track of your daily, weekly, and monthly schedule. You can quickly add appointments to your schedule planner using the Appointment form, which includes fields for entering details about the appointment, when and where it takes place, and how long it lasts.

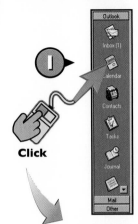

Click

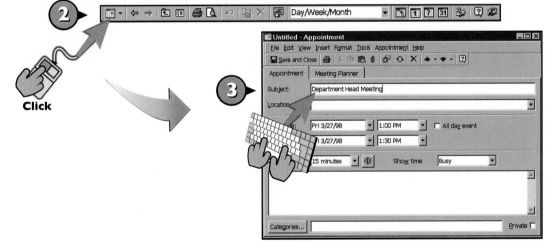

Click

✓ Scheduling Events

Need to schedule an all-day event in your calendar? Select the **All day event** check box in the Appointment form. This marks your appointment as an all-day event in your calendar, placing the appointment subject title at the top of the daily view schedule.

① ▶ Click the **Calendar** icon on the Outlook Bar to open the Calendar folder.

② ▶ Click the **New Appointment** button on the Outlook toolbar.

③ ▶ Click in the **Subject** field and type a title for your appointment. Press **Tab** or click in the next field and continue filling in information as needed.

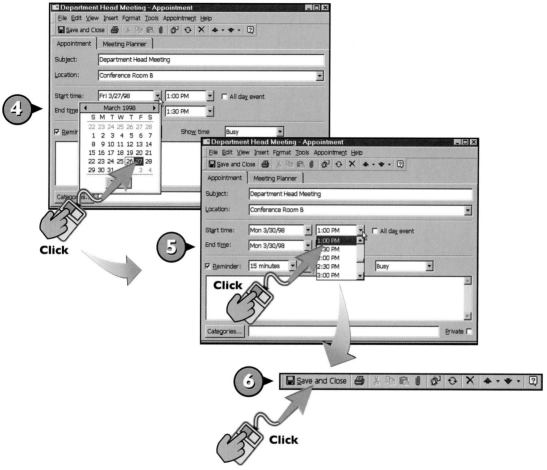

Click

Click

4 ▶ Click the **date** drop-down list and choose a date.

5 ▶ Click the **time** drop-down list to select a start time and end time.

6 ▶ Click **Save and Close** to add the appointment to your calendar.

✅ **Changing the Time Increment**
As you work with the Appointment form, you may notice that Outlook assigns a default time of 30 minutes to an appointment. Use the **End time** drop-down list to lengthen or shorten the time span.

End
Task

Scheduling Recurring Appointments

If your schedule has a lot of recurring appointments, such as weekly sales meetings, you don't have to enter in each meeting as an individual appointment— use Outlook's Recurring Appointment feature to schedule repeating appointments for you. You can specify the recurrence pattern, whether the appointment is weekly or monthly, what day of the week it falls on, and when the appointment starts and ends.

Task 24: Creating Recurring Appointments

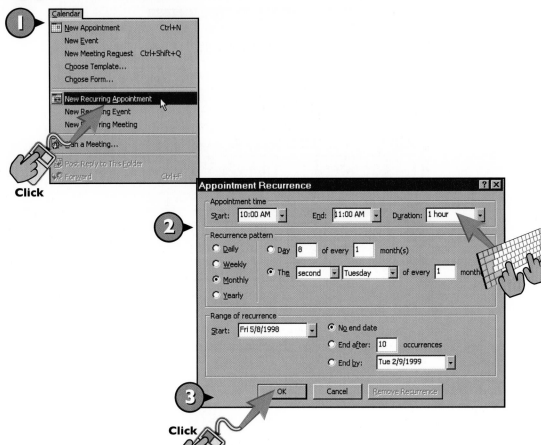

✓ Open the Calendar Folder

Switch to the Calendar folder to set recurring appointments. Click the **Calendar** icon in the Outlook Bar.

1 Choose **Calendar**, **New Recurring Appointment** from the menu bar.

2 In the Appointment Recurrence dialog box, fill out the information about this recurring date, such as start and end times, and the pattern of recurrence.

3 Click **OK** to open the Appointment form.

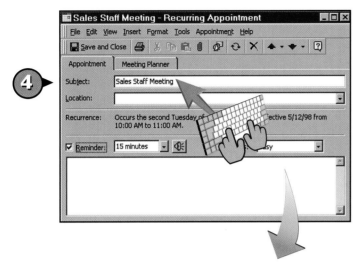

Click

✅ **Options Will Vary**
Depending on what recurrence pattern you select, the options in the Appointment Recurrence dialog box will change to reflect the type of pattern. For example, if you choose Monthly, you can specify on which day of the month the appointment falls.

✅ **Editing Existing Appointments**
To turn an appointment you've already created into a recurring appointment, double-click the appointment from the calendar and click the **Recurrence** button on the Appointment form toolbar. This opens the Appointment Recurrence dialog box, and you can now designate how often the appointment occurs. Click **OK** to return to the Appointment form, then click **Save and Close**.

④ An Appointment form opens with the information about the recurring dates already filled in. Enter the **Subject** and **Location** information.

⑤ Click **Save and Close**.

Task 25: Viewing Your Schedule

Changing the Calendar View

Outlook's Calendar folder is designed to look like a daily planner. But unlike paper-based planner notebooks, Outlook's Calendar folder lets you instantly change the way you view your schedule. You can choose to view your schedule by day, week, or month, among other view options.

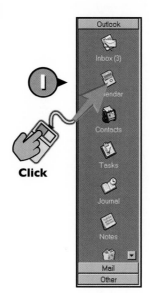

Start Here

Click

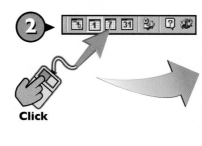

Click

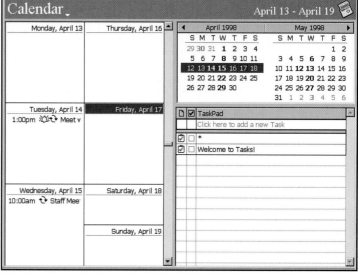

✅ **Default View**
When you first use Calendar, you start out in Day/Week/Month view, but you can easily change the view using the **Current View** drop-down list on the Outlook toolbar. Simply click the drop-down arrow and choose a new view.

1 ▸ Open the Calendar folder by clicking the **Calendar** icon on the Outlook Bar.

2 ▸ Use the **Day**, **Week**, and **Month** buttons on the toolbar to change your schedule display. For example, click the **Week** button to see your schedule presented in a week format.

Next Step ▸

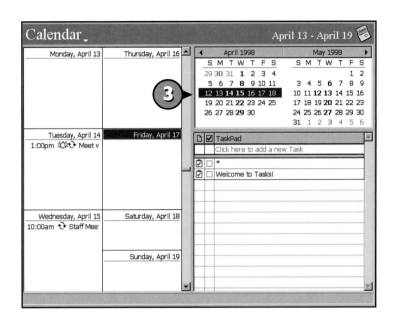

Click

 Use the Monthly calendar pane available in Day and Week view to change which dates are displayed. Click the date or week you want to view.

 Use the arrows to scroll to other months in the Monthly calendar pane.

 Current Date
As you work with the Monthly calendar pane to choose new dates to view, it always points out the current date with a red box around it.

 What's Today?
To quickly find the current day in your daily schedule, click the **Go To Today** button on the Outlook toolbar.

End Task

Task 26: Creating Folders

Adding Folders

All the components in Outlook are folders, and your Inbox, Sent Items box, and other mailboxes are also folders. You can create additional folders to keep mail or other Outlook items together. Perhaps you want to save things by project, or separate personal and business items.

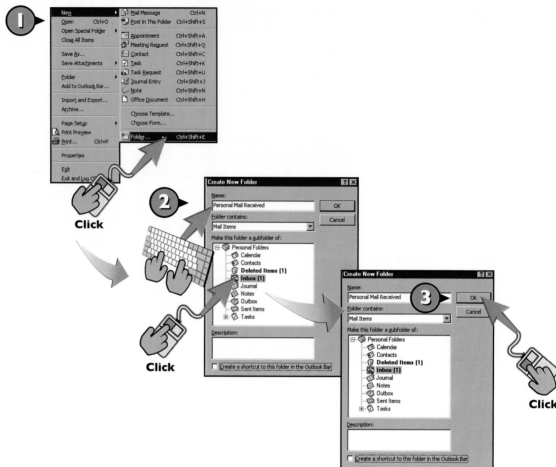

Start Here

Click

Click

Click

✅ **Avoid Overcrowding**
When you're creating a folder, Outlook puts a shortcut to the folder on the Outlook Bar. However, unless you think you'll be opening the folder constantly, or dragging items to it, it's probably better to avoid crowding the Outlook Bar. In the Create New Folder dialog box, make sure the **Create a shortcut to this folder in the Outlook Bar** check box is deselected.

1 Choose **File**, **New**, **Folder** from the menu bar.

2 In the Create New Folder dialog box, give your new folder a name. Then select the folder that will hold your new folder (called the parent folder).

3 Choose **OK**.

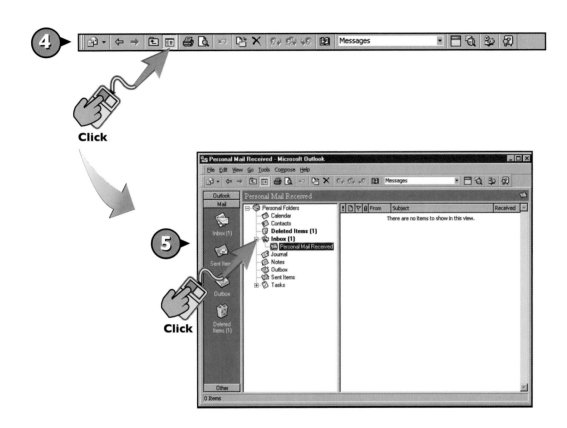

Click

Click

Viewing Your Folder List

You can view Outlook's Folder List from any of the components. Just click on the Folder List button on the Outlook toolbar.

Resizing the Folder List

If you're having trouble seeing your Folder List, you can resize the right border of the list by moving your pointer over the border until it takes the shape of a double-sided arrow. Then press and hold the mouse button and drag the border to the right to widen it. When you release the mouse button, the Folder List is expanded.

4 To see your folder, click the **Folder list** icon on the toolbar.

5 Click the **plus sign** next to the parent folder to see your new folder.

Task 27: Moving Items into Folders

Organizing Folder Items

You can move any item from one folder to another, which is extremely useful if you're organizing everything by project, or you need to separate personal and business items. This works for mail, contacts, tasks, or any other Outlook item.

✓ Folder Shortcut

When you open the Move to Folder menu, a list of recently used folders appears. Select the one you need, and the item is moved immediately.

✓ Using Drag and Drop

If you're a confident mouse user, another way to move items from folder to folder is to drag and drop them. Select the item you want to move, press and hold the mouse button, drag the item to a new folder on the Outlook Bar, release the mouse button, and the item is moved.

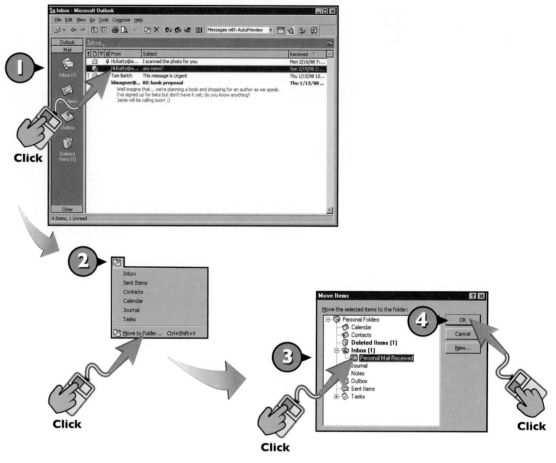

Click

Click

Click

Click

1. Select the item you want to move.

2. Click the **Move to Folder** button on the Outlook toolbar. From the drop-down menu that appears, choose **Move to Folder**.

3. Select a folder to hold this item.

4. Choose **OK**, and the item is moved.

Task 28: Using Sticky Notes

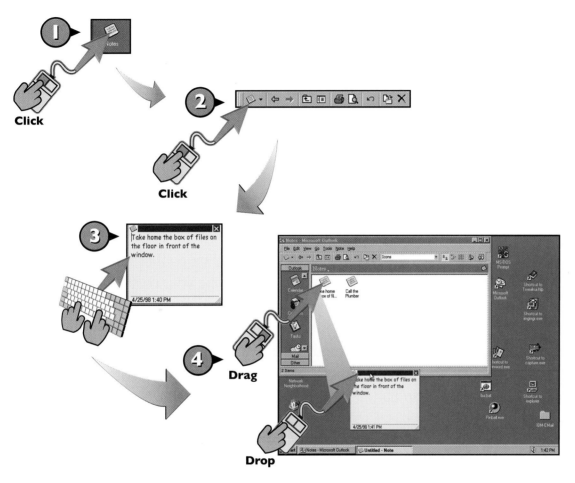

Click

Click

 Drag

Drop

Using the Notes Folder

Outlook's Notes folder provides you with the electronic equivalent of sticky notes. You can write yourself reminders, jot down important instructions, or type any kind of note to yourself. You can place sticky notes on your Windows desktop, or visit the Notes folder to read them.

 Click the **Notes** icon on the Outlook Bar to move to the Notes window.

 Click the **New Note** button on the toolbar.

 Write yourself a note! Outlook takes care of the date and time.

 You can drag the note to your desktop for a constant reminder (a copy remains in the Outlook Notes folder).

 Reading Notes
To read a note from the Notes folder, double-click on the note's icon. To close it again, click anywhere outside the note or press the Esc key.

Publisher

Microsoft Publisher 98 is a desktop publishing tool designed to help you create polished, professional publications. It comes with a vast assortment of publications for every occasion; all you have to do is choose a design and fill in your own text. For example, you can produce quality newsletters, brochures, business cards, letterhead and matching envelopes, flyers and advertisements, even Web pages—and that's just the tip of the iceberg. Forget about agonizing over designs and layouts; let Publisher do all the hard work for you. It's like having a professional printing service inside your computer.

In this part of the book, you learn the basics for building publications out of text and picture frames, including using clip art and drawing your own shapes. Half the battle of creating any publication is figuring out what the design and layout should be; but with Publisher's premade publications and wizards that walk through each step of the process, the battle is already fought. The only thing that remains is entering your own text, and Publisher is even willing to help you with that. Click on Publisher's Show Help button for instant assistance with any aspect of your publication.

If premade publications aren't for you, you can also design your own from scratch. Use what you learn about inserting and manipulating frames in this part of the book to whip up your own standout publications.

Tasks

Task 1: Starting a New Publication

Using the Catalog

Files you create in Publisher 98 are called publications. When you first open Publisher, the Catalog box appears with a variety of publication choices, much like a directory. You can start a new publication and use a wizard to help build it, open an existing publication, or build your own publication from scratch. The Catalog tabs organize the various choices.

✓ Opening the Catalog

To start a new file from the Publisher program window, open the **File** menu and select **New**. This displays the Catalog box, and you can choose a publication wizard to use.

✓ Using Wizards

The easiest way to create a publication is to use a wizard to walk you through each step. Task 2 shows you how.

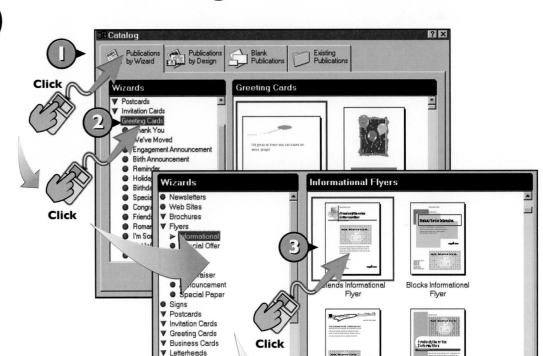

1. From the Catalog, click the tab you want to view, such as **Publications by Wizard**.

2. The list on the left side displays available publications. Click on the publication you're interested in.

3. The list on the right side displays the available styles for the publication you select. Click on the style you want to use.

4. To begin the wizard, click the **Start Wizard** button.

Task 2: Creating Publications with Wizards

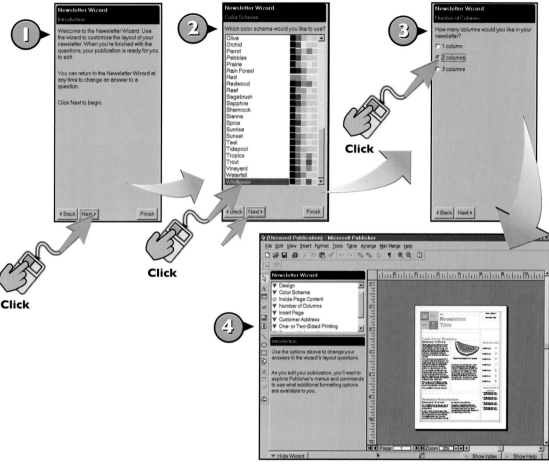

1 Click

Click

Click

4

3 Click

Walking Through the Wizard Steps

The easiest way to create a publication is to use one of Publisher's wizards. A wizard will take you through each step in building your publication by asking questions. You supply your answers regarding the options available for the type of publication you selected. At the end of the steps, you end up with a layout ready to be filled in with text.

✓ **Different Steps**
Depending on the publication you choose, the wizard steps and questions will vary.

✓ **Hiding the Wizard**
You can hide the wizard to free up more space onscreen for viewing the publication. Click the **Hide Wizard** button on the status bar. To redisplay the wizard again, click the **Show Wizard** button.

1 The first wizard box introduces you to the wizard. Click **Next** to continue.

2 The wizard presents a series of questions, each requiring a specific type of answer. Answer the question, then click **Next** to continue.

3 The wizard may present options you can choose from. Click the option, then click **Next**.

4 At the final wizard step, click the **Finish** button. The publication is generated and the wizard remains open.

End Task

Task 3: Zooming In and Out

Using the F9 Key

By default, Publisher 98 opens your publication in a zoomed out view so you can keep an eye on the overall picture. However, it's difficult to view headings and text at this zoom level, particularly when you start typing in text. You can quickly zoom in and out using the **F9** key on the keyboard.

Other Zoom Tools

If you prefer a tailor-made zoom, open the **View** menu, select **Zoom**, and choose a zoom percentage to use. You can also find **Zoom** tools on the status bar. Click the **Zoom Out** or **Zoom In** buttons next to the **Zoom** percentage box to change your view.

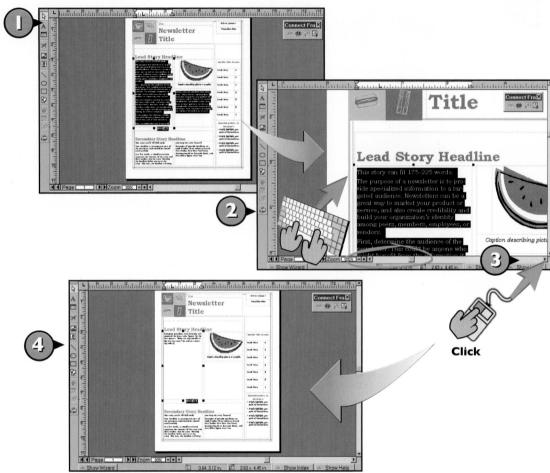

Click

1 ▶ When you click a text box and begin entering your own words, you can't see what you're typing.

2 ▶ Press **F9** to zoom in up close and personal.

3 ▶ Use the scroll bars and arrows to move to the appropriate position on the page.

4 ▶ When you finish typing, press **F9** again. This zooms you back to see the overall effect.

Task 4: Replacing Placeholder Text

Start Here

Click

Click

Entering Your Own Text

Your publication layout emerges from the wizard steps with headlines and body copy already inserted. This is *placeholder text*. You must enter your own text to begin filling in your publication. All the text is enclosed in text boxes, called frames. You must select each text frame to enter or edit text.

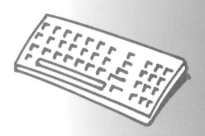

① Click anywhere in a text frame to highlight the placeholder text.

② Enter your own text. As soon as you enter the first character, the highlighted text disappears.

③ Click anywhere outside the publication page to deselect the text frame.

✓ **Use F9 to Zoom**
Press **F9** on the keyboard to quickly zoom in and out to view your publication.

End Task

Task 5: Moving Through Pages

Viewing Pages

Unlike most of the other Windows software you use, you cannot use the scroll bars to move from page to page in Publisher 98. The scroll bars only move you up and down and side-to-side on the page that is currently in the Publisher window. You must use the page controls located to the left of the horizontal scroll bar to move through pages.

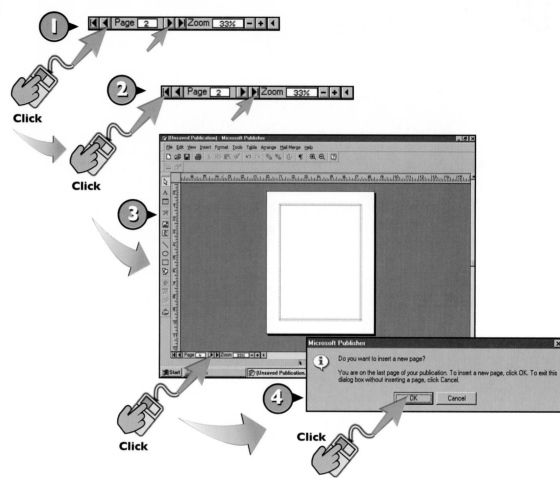

① Use the arrows next to the page number to move ahead or back one page at a time.

② Click the arrows farthest from the page number to move to the first page or last page of your publication.

③ When you are working on the last page, click the **Next Page** arrow to add another page.

④ A prompt box appears. Click **OK** to add a page.

Task 6: Working with Two-Page Spreads

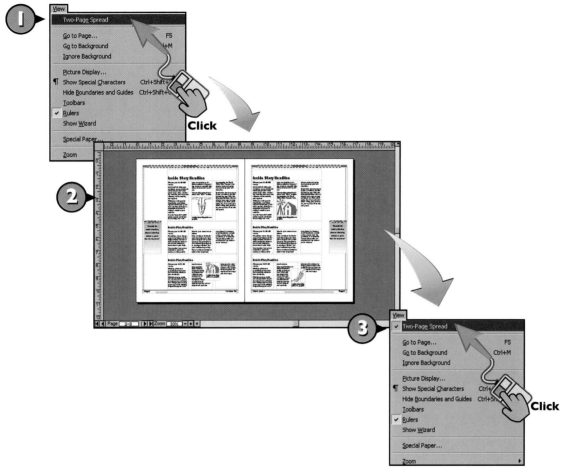

Viewing a Two-Page Spread

By default, Publisher 98 lets you view single pages. If you're designing a publication of four pages that is printed on both sides of the paper, you can work in two-page mode to get a better idea of the layout. Use Publisher's **View** menu to help you make the switch.

Click

Click

1 ▶ Open the **View** menu and choose **Two-Page Spread**.

2 ▶ Your publication displays side-by-side pages. If you are working on page 1 or page 4, you see a single page because there's nothing to the left of the page or to the right of the back page.

3 ▶ To return to single-page view, open the **View** menu again and choose **Two-Page Spread**.

✓ **Left or Right?**
When you design any type of newsletter or booklet with multiple pages printed on both sides of the paper, the odd pages are always on the right and the even pages are always on the left.

Task 7: Saving Your Publication

Using the Save Command

As with any file you work on, it's a good idea to save frequently in case of a power outage or computer glitch. Unlike the other Office programs, Publisher 98 even prompts you to save with a prompt box every 15 minutes. For a traditional save, use the **Save** command and assign a name to the file. Regardless of when you save, the Save As dialog box appears when you first assign a filename to the publication.

✓ Changing the Save Prompt

To change the amount of time between prompts to save, open the **Tools** menu and select **Options**. Click the **Editing and User Assistance** tab and enter a new time increment in the **Minutes between reminders** text box. Click **OK** to exit.

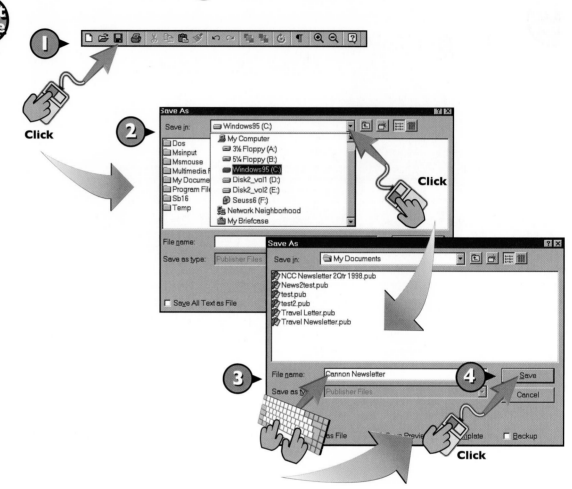

① Click the **Save** button on the toolbar.

② The first time you save a publication, the Save As dialog box opens. Locate the folder where you want to save the publication using the **Save in** drop-down list.

③ Enter a name for the file in the **File name** text box. (Publisher automatically adds the extension .pub for you.)

④ Click **Save**.

Task 8: Opening a Saved Publication

Start Here

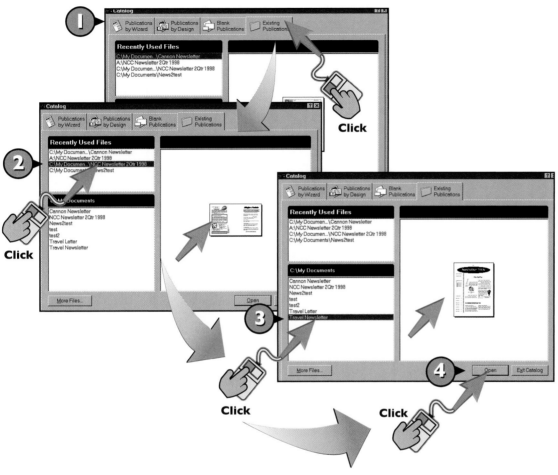

Click

Click

Click

Click

Using the Existing Publications Tab

After you save a publication, you'll probably want to open it again at a later time to work on it. Use the **Existing Publications** tab in the **Catalog** to locate the file you want to open. The tab lists recently used files as well as other publication files you've saved.

✓ **One File at a Time**
Unlike other Windows programs, you can open only one file at a time in Publisher 98.

✓ **Other File Opening Routes**
If you click the **Open** button on the toolbar, the Open Publication dialog box appears instead. Choose **Open** to open the publication.

✓ **Quick Open**
If you don't need to preview the file in Catalog before opening it, double-click on the filename and Publisher quickly opens the publication.

1 From the Catalog, click the **Existing Publications** tab.

2 Check the **Recently Used Files** list if you recently worked on the file. If the file you want is listed, select it to see a preview.

3 You can also look in the folder list to locate a file. Select a file to see a preview.

4 After locating and selecting the file you want to open, click the **Open** button.

End Task

Task 9: Creating a Publication by Design

Using Publisher's Design Sets

Besides all the great publications you can create with Publisher's wizards, you can also choose to create items designed to go together. You might want your business card to match your envelopes, or your fax cover sheet to match your letterhead. You can use Publisher's Design Sets to create sets of related business publications that use the same design for an overall professional look.

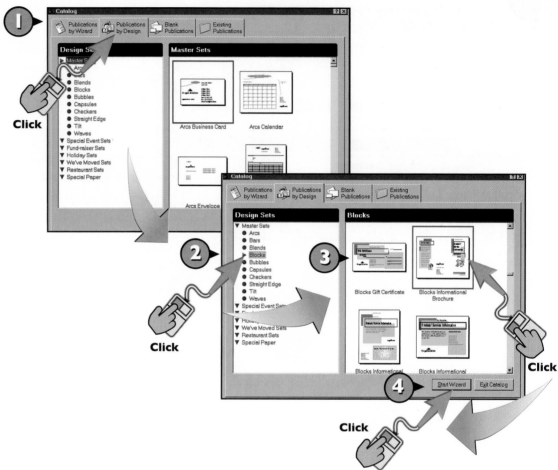

✓ **Check Them Out!**
You'll find plenty of fun design sets in addition to business sets in the **Publications by Design** tab, such as holiday sets, special events sets, and more.

---

1 From the Catalog, click on the **Publications by Design** tab.

2 Select a design from the **Design Sets** list.

3 Choose a publication type.

4 Click the **Start Wizard** button to open the publication.

Task 10: Creating a New Publication from Scratch

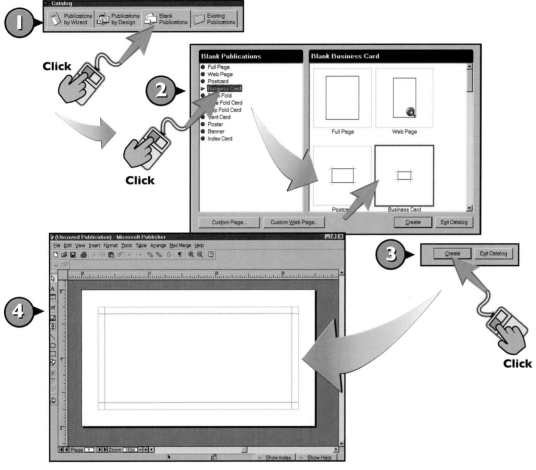

Click

Click

Click

Start Here

Starting a Blank Presentation

If you're really adventurous, you can choose to create a publication from scratch, foregoing Publisher 98's vast selection of publications. You can easily do this from Publisher's Catalog and the Blank Publications tab. Pick a page size, and an empty publication is yours to build on.

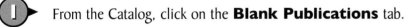

1. From the Catalog, click on the **Blank Publications** tab.

2. Select the type of page you want to create from the **Blank Publications** list, and the right list box shows a simulated size.

3. Click the **Create** button.

4. A blank publication opens ready to be filled with text and graphic frames, as needed.

✅ Quick Open
If you don't need to preview the blank publication page before opening it, double-click on the publication, and Publisher quickly opens it.

✅ Display the Catalog
If you've already launched Publisher, select **File, Open** to display the Catalog again.

End Task

Task 11: Creating a Text Frame

Working with Text Frames

You can't just start typing on the page to begin entering text in Publisher. Every element in your publication, including text, must have a frame. A frame is simply a box designated for text or graphics. All the Wizard publications have premade text frames ready to go, but there may be times when you need to add your own, particularly if you create a blank publication.

✓ Deleting Frames
If you don't like the text frame you created and want to start over, select the frame and press the **Del** key to erase it.

✓ Using the Objects Toolbar
The Objects toolbar works like any other toolbar; it's just vertical instead of horizontal. To learn what each button is, hover your mouse pointer over the button and read the ScreenTip.

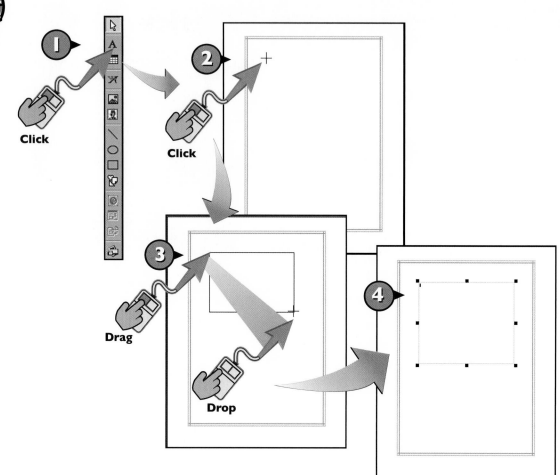

Start Here

Click

Click

Drag

Drop

1 ► Click the **Text Frame Tool** on the Objects toolbar.

2 ► Position your pointer where you want to position the upper-left corner of the text frame.

3 ► Hold down the left mouse button and drag down and to the right until the frame is the size you want.

4 ► Release the mouse button, and the frame is set.

End Task

Task 12: Adding Text to a Text Frame

Start Here

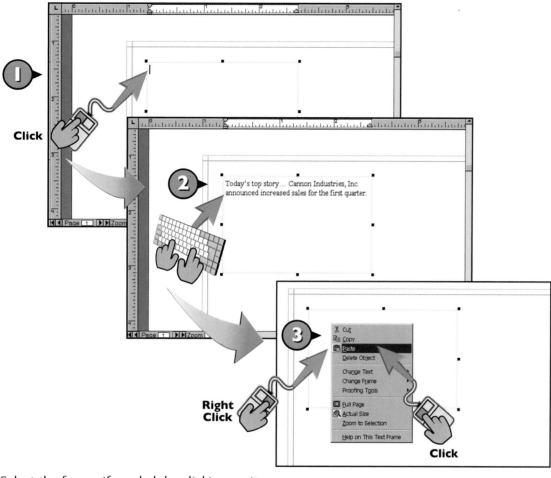

Click

Right Click

Click

Entering Text

After you create a text frame, you can fill it with text. Click inside and start typing, or copy text from other programs into the frame.

✓ **Don't Forget the F9 Key!**
Press **F9** on the keyboard to zoom in and get a better look at what you're typing.

✓ **Selecting Frames**
To select a frame, click on it. A grayed line border surrounds the frame and its selection handles (tiny black boxes) appear active.

✓ **Copying and Pasting Text**
Use the universal **Copy** command to copy text from another application to place in a Publisher text frame. Select the text in the application, choose **Edit, Copy, Return to Publisher**, and you're ready to paste it in place.

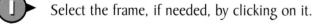

1 ▶ Select the frame, if needed, by clicking on it.

2 ▶ The cursor is in position, blinking and ready to go. Start entering your text.

3 ▶ If you've copied text from a word processing document, right-click in the text frame and choose **Paste Text** from the Shortcut menu.

End Task

Task 13: Formatting Text

Using Publisher's Formatting Tools

Publisher provides a full range of formatting tools for manipulating the text you place in your publication. When you click on a text frame, the Formatting toolbar displays text formatting buttons.

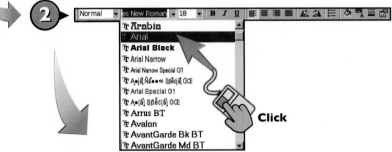

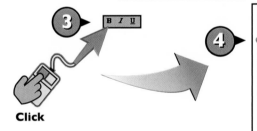

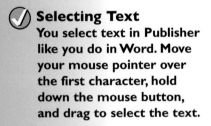

Selecting Text

You select text in Publisher like you do in Word. Move your mouse pointer over the first character, hold down the mouse button, and drag to select the text.

More Formatting Options

To find more formatting options, open the **Format** menu and select **Font**. This opens the Font dialog box where you can find additional formatting controls.

 Select the text you want to format.

 Use the tools on the Formatting toolbar to change the appearance of the selected text. To change the Font, click on the **Font** drop-down arrow and select a new font.

 To make the text bold, click the **Bold** button.

 The formatting is applied to the text.

Task 14: Moving and Resizing Text Frames

Start Here

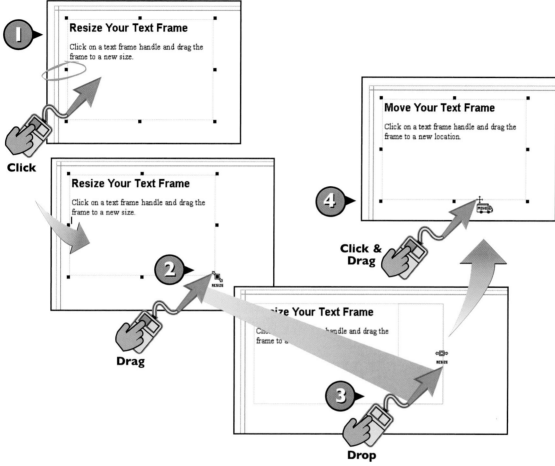

Click

Resize Your Text Frame

Click on a text frame handle and drag the frame to a new size.

Drag

Resize Your Text Frame

Click on a text frame handle and drag the frame to a new size.

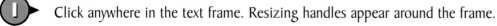
Resize Your Text Frame

Cli... ...handle and drag the frame to a...

Drop

Move Your Text Frame

Click on a text frame handle and drag the frame to a new location.

Click & Drag

Moving and Resizing with the Mouse

You can easily move and resize your text frames as needed using your mouse. When you select a frame, it's surrounded by tiny black boxes called handles. You can drag any of the handles to resize the frame.

✓ **Keeping Proportions**
When you resize a text frame, you can keep the proportions intact by holding down **Shift** as you drag a corner handle. Release the mouse button before you let go of the **Shift** button.

✓ **Resizing Tip**
Use a corner handle if you want to change two sides of the frame at once while you drag.

✓ **How to Drag**
Hold down the left mouse button, move the mouse until the frame reaches the desired size or location, then release the mouse button.

1 Click anywhere in the text frame. Resizing handles appear around the frame.

2 To change the size of the frame, move your pointer to any sizing handle (the pointer changes to a Resize pointer). Drag the sizing handle in the appropriate direction.

3 Release the mouse button, and the frame is resized.

4 To move the frame, position your pointer so it turns into a moving van, then drag to a new location.

End Task

Task 15: Handling Overflow Text

Using Multiple Frames

When there's more text than fits in a frame, it's called overflow text. The text is still there, you just can't see it. Publisher holds the extra text in an Overflow area and lets you know with the Text in Overflow indicator button at the bottom of the text frame. Use the Connecting tools to connect frames and place the overflow text.

✓ **Just a Little Too Much?**
If your overflow text is only a word or sentence, try reducing the font size or resizing the frame.

✓ **Unconnecting Frames**
To unconnect frames, select the first frame, then click the **Disconnect Text Frames** button on the floating Connect Frames toolbar.

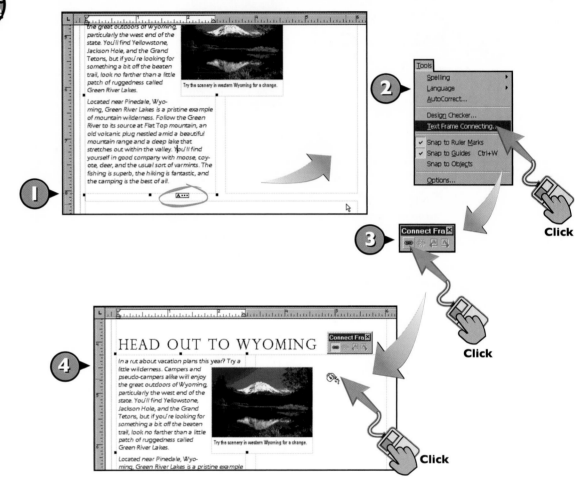

1 When there's more text than fits in the frame, Publisher displays the frame's connect button, which displays three dots.

2 Open the **Tools** menu and select **Text Frame Connecting**.

3 Click the **Connect Text Frames** button on the Connect Frames toolbar, and your pointer turns into a pitcher.

4 Move to another text frame and click to "pour" the overflow text into the frame.

Task 16: Adding a Picture Frame

Start Here

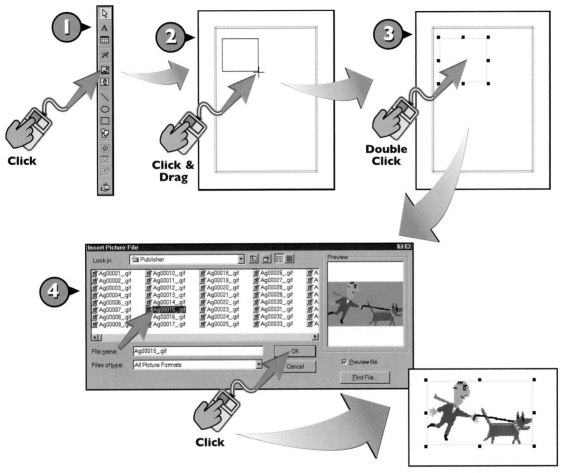

Click

Click & Drag

Double Click

Click

Working with Picture Frames

Like text, all graphics you place in a publication must appear in frames, called *picture frames*. Many of the publications you create using wizards already come with picture frames ready to fill, but there are times when you want to add your own picture frames, especially if you're creating a publication from scratch. After you create a picture frame, you can fill it with clip art, a graphic created from another program, or a photograph that's been scanned in.

✅ **Finding Graphics**
You can import graphics or use Publisher's collection of clip art and photographs.

✅ **Quick Frame**
To quickly insert a default-size picture frame, select the **Picture Frame Tool** and double-click in your publication.

① Click the **Picture Frame Tool** button on the Objects toolbar.

② Position your pointer where you want the upper-left corner to appear then drag down and to the right to create the frame.

③ Double-click inside the frame.

④ Select the graphic you want to use and click **OK** to insert the picture.

End Task

Task 17: Moving and Resizing Picture Frames

Moving and Resizing with the Mouse

You can easily move and resize picture and clip art frames with your mouse. When you select a frame, it's surrounded by tiny black squares called sizing handles. Use the handles to resize the frame. Use the frame's border to move the frame.

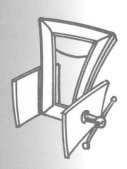

✓ Maintaining Proportions

Sometimes resizing distorts the picture (although occasionally that's an effective technique), so you should hold down the **Shift** key while you're dragging to maintain proportions.

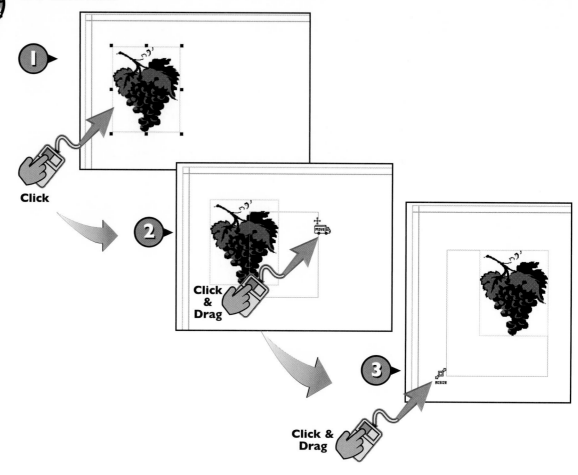

Start Here

Click

1

Click & Drag

2

Click & Drag

3

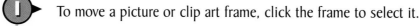

1 To move a picture or clip art frame, click the frame to select it.

2 When your pointer turns into a moving van, drag the frame to its new position.

3 To resize a frame, move the pointer over a sizing handle; the pointer changes to a Resize pointer. Drag the resizing handle to enlarge or shrink the frame.

End Task

Task 18: Inserting WordArt

Start Here

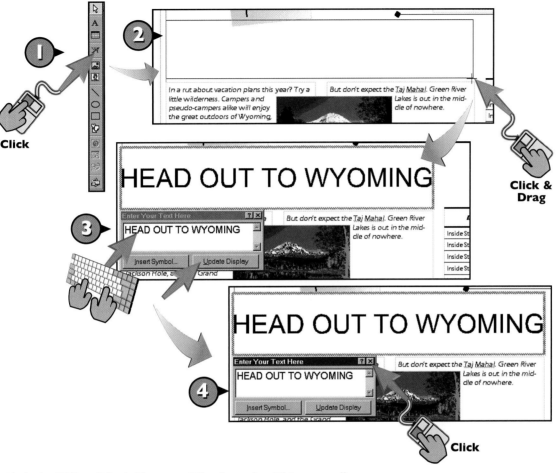

Click

Click & Drag

Click

What's WordArt?

Use Publisher's WordArt feature to turn text into graphics. You can apply WordArt's special effects to twist, curve, and embellish words and phrases to make them stand out on the page.

1. Click the **WordArt Frame Tool** on the Objects toolbar.

2. Drag to create a WordArt frame of the size you need.

3. When you release the mouse button, the WordArt dialog box opens. Enter your text and click **Update Display**.

4. Click the **Close** button, and you're ready to format the text as explained in Part 4, Task 19.

End Task

Task 19: Formatting WordArt

Adding Special Effects

After you've entered your WordArt text, as explained in Task 18, you can use all the tools on the WordArt toolbar to create special effects, such as wavy, curved, and tilted text. You can also add shadows and shading. Use these effects to create standout text in your publication.

✅ Selecting WordArt Frames

There are two ways to select WordArt frames. Single-click to select the frame normally (a border and resizing handles) so you can move or resize it. Double-click to place a hash-mark border around the frame, which means you can format the WordArt text.

✅ Exiting WordArt

To close the WordArt toolbar, click anywhere outside the WordArt frame on the publication.

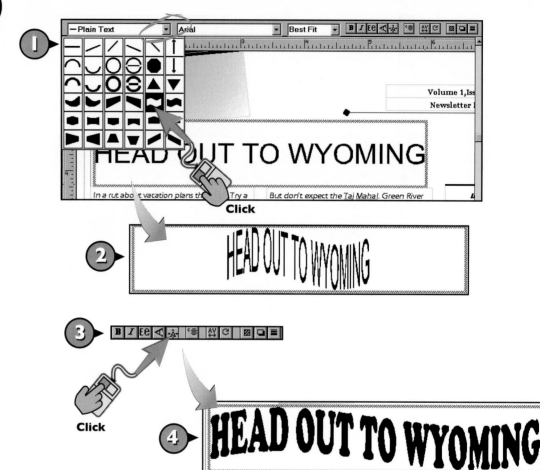

1. With the WordArt frame selected, click the arrow next to the **Shape** box on the WordArt toolbar and select a shape.

2. Your text takes the shape of the effect you selected.

3. To stretch out your text in the frame, click the **Stretch** button on the toolbar.

4. WordArt stretches your text. Continue applying effects to get the look you want.

Task 20: Putting a Picture Frame in a Text Frame

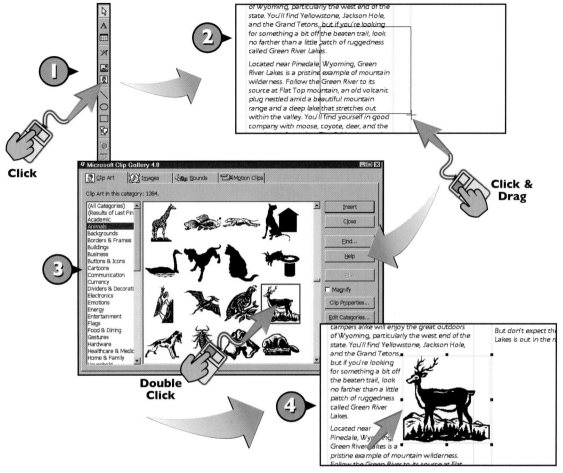

Click

Click & Drag

Double Click

Inserting Frames into Frames

To illustrate a story or article, you can put a picture right into the text frame that holds the text. This is often more compelling than having the picture in a separate frame above or below the text frame.

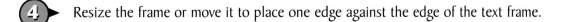

1. Click the **Clip Gallery Tool** button on the Objects toolbar.

2. Click the pointer where you want to start the frame, then drag to create the frame.

3. The Clip Gallery dialog box appears. Double-click the clip art you want to use.

4. Resize the frame or move it to place one edge against the edge of the text frame.

✓ **Wrapping Text**
After you insert a picture frame into a text frame, you can use Publisher's wrap tools to wrap text around the object, as explained in Part 4, Task 21.

End Task

Task 21: Wrapping Text Around a Frame

Working with the Wrap Controls

After you've inserted a graphic frame in a text frame, the text wraps around the frame, not the artwork. If it's done properly, this can look very professional. If you prefer, you can also wrap text around the artwork. Use Publisher's wrap controls to create the effect you want.

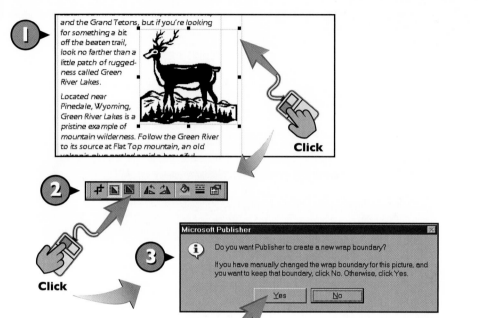

 Select the picture frame around which you want to wrap text.

 Click the **Wrap Text to Picture** button.

 Publisher offers to create a new wrap boundary; click **Yes**.

Publisher offers to create a new wrap boundary; click **Yes**.

The text wraps around the artwork. You may have some text cut off that you need to fix.

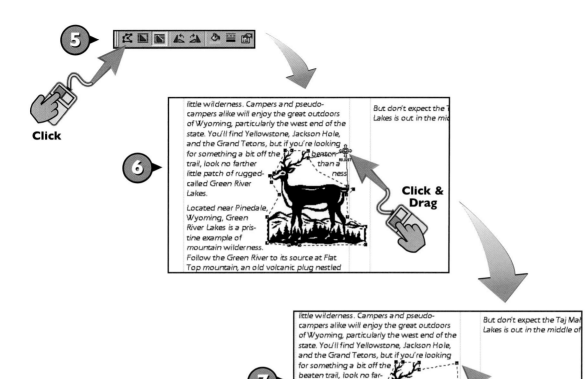

Click

Click & Drag

5 ▶ Click the **Edit Irregular Wrap** button.

6 ▶ Drag a handle to move the wrap frame outward to push back any text or drag a handle inward to create a better wrap.

7 ▶ Move as many handles as needed to create the effect you want.

End Task

Task 22: Printing a Publication

Using the Print Options

Publisher offers several ways to transfer your publication to the printed page. You can print it the same way you print other documents using the **Print** command. Or you can prepare your publication for an outside, professional printer. For example, if you create a brochure, you can take it to a professional printing service.

✅ Quick Print

To print without checking the Printer options, click the **Print** button on the Standard toolbar.

✅ Preparing for Outside Printing

Open the **File** menu and select **Prepare File for Printing Service, Set Up Publication.** A set of dialog boxes helps you prepare the publication. Select the appropriate options and click **Next.** At the last step, click **Done.**

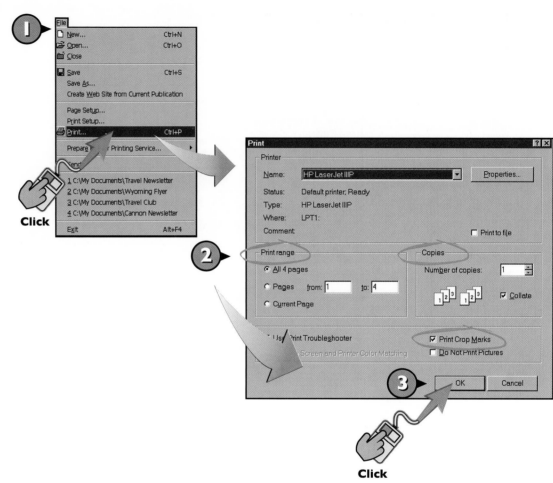

 Open the **File** menu and select **Print**.

 In the Print dialog box, make any necessary changes to the print options.

 Click **OK** to print the publication.

End
Task

Task 23: Inserting a Simple Shape

Start Here

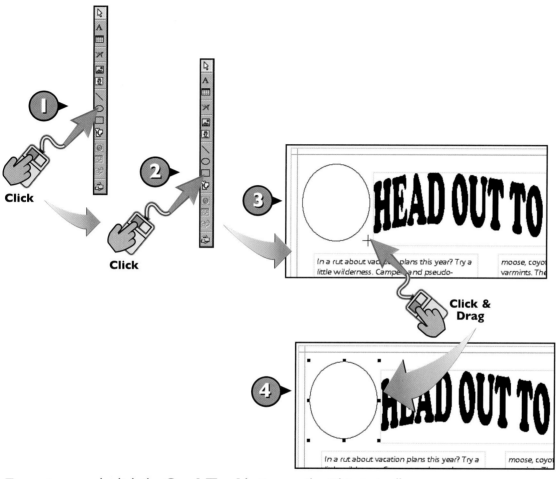

Click

Click

Click & Drag

Working with Shapes

Shapes can be used in a publication to draw attention to important headings or text. You can place text over shapes, stack shapes to create drawings, and more. Use Publisher's **Oval** and **Rectangle** tools to create circles, ovals, squares, and rectangles. Like frames, shapes can be resized and moved around in the publication.

✅ **Perfect Shapes**
To draw a perfect circle or square, hold down the **Shift** key while you drag the mouse.

✅ **Resizing Shapes**
To resize a shape, click it to display its sizing handles, and drag a handle. To move a shape, drag its border.

1. To create an oval, click the **Oval Tool** button on the Objects toolbar.

2. To create a rectangle, click the **Rectangle Tool** on the Objects toolbar.

3. Place your pointer where you want to insert the shape and drag your mouse to create the shape you need.

4. Release the mouse button, and the shape is created.

End Task

Task 24: Inserting a Custom Shape

Using the Custom Shapes Tool

Aside from the standard ovals and rectangles, you can also draw more elaborate shapes in Publisher. Use the **Custom Shapes** tool to create starbursts, arrows, octagons, and more.

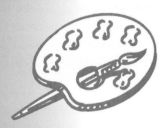

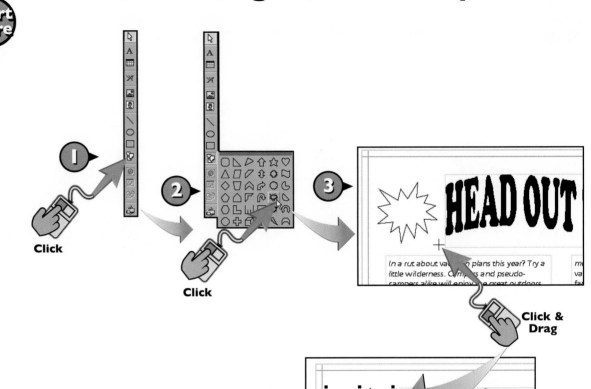

Click

Click

Click & Drag

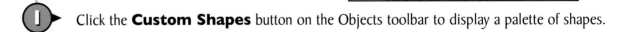

✓ Resizing Shapes

To resize a shape, click on it to display its sizing handles, and drag a handle. To move a shape, drag its border.

✓ Drawing Perfect Shapes

To draw a perfectly proportioned shape, hold down the **Shift** key while you drag the mouse.

1 Click the **Custom Shapes** button on the Objects toolbar to display a palette of shapes.

2 Click on the shape you want to draw.

3 Click in the publication where you want the shape placed, then drag to draw the desired size.

4 Release the mouse button and the shape is created.

End Task

Task 25: Adding Color and Texture to Shapes

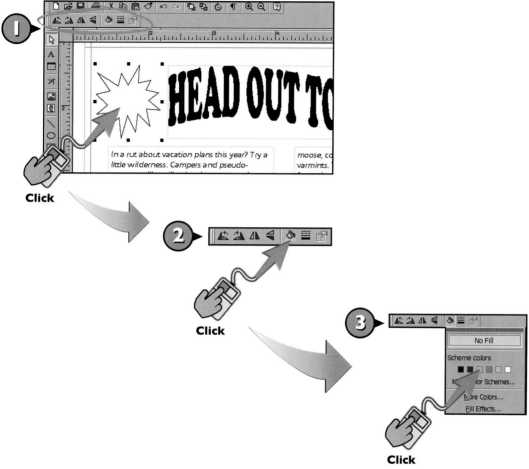

Click

Click

Click

Start Here

1. Click the shape to select it. This causes the **Graphics** buttons to appear on the Formatting toolbar.

2. Click the **Fill Color** button on the Formatting toolbar.

3. Click a color, and it's added to your shape. (To choose from a more varied color palette, choose **More Colors**.)

Using the Fill Color Tool

To give the shapes you add to your publication some personality and pizzazz, apply color, shading, and patterns. When you colorize shapes, the colors available in your color scheme are offered, but you can also choose to see other color schemes or the full range of available colors.

✓ Using Colors with Frames
The color and texture techniques discussed here for shapes work on all types of frames in Publisher 98.

✓ Adding Texture
To add texture, choose **Fill Effects** from the Fill Color palette to open the Fill Effects dialog box. Select **Patterns** (lines form a design) or **Gradients** (shades of color). Choose **OK** to exit.

Task 26: Grouping Objects

Using the Group Objects Feature

You can group several objects together and treat them as one object. When items are grouped, they can be moved or resized together, rather than separately. For example, you can group a text frame, a picture frame, and a shape frame to form one object.

✓ **Locking and Unlocking Groups**
When the **Group Objects** button appears unlocked, the grouping isn't permanent. However, it remains a group until you click outside it. To lock a group, click on the **Group Objects** button. To unlock, click the **Ungroup Objects** button.

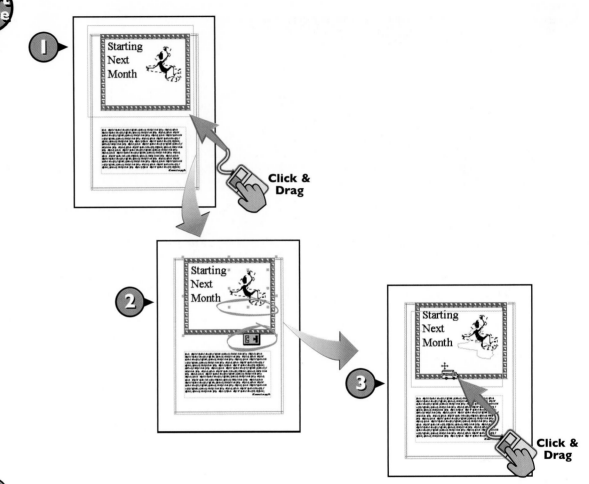

Start Here

Click & Drag

Click & Drag

1. Hold down the left mouse button and drag to draw a box around the elements you want to group together.

2. When you release the mouse, you see grayed-out sizing handles for each element and a **Group Objects** button at the bottom of the enclosed group.

3. To move the group, position your mouse at any point in the group where the pointer turns into a moving van, and drag the group to a new position.

End Task

Task 27: Working with Borders

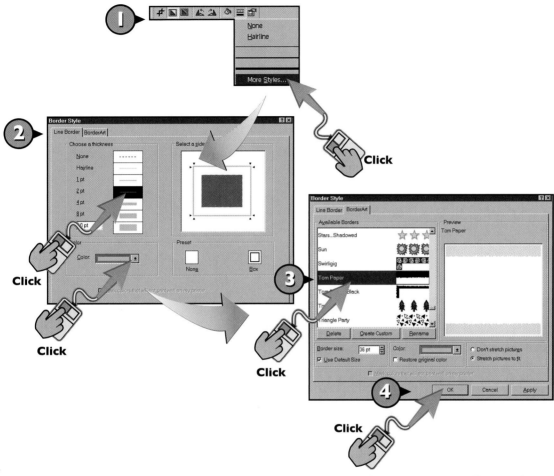

Using the Border Tool

When you hang pictures on the wall, the frame you choose can enhance the picture, the wall, and the room. The same thing is true of the elements in your publication. Frame your text and graphic elements to make your publication more interesting and professional. Use the **Border** tool to add borders that set off headlines and important text, or make graphics more distinguished.

① Select the frame, click the **Line/Border Style** button on the Formatting toolbar, and then click **More Styles**.

② Use the **Line Border** tab to set a custom line thickness and color.

③ Use the **BorderArt** tab to select an ornate border. You can even specify size and color.

④ Click **OK** to exit the dialog box and apply the border.

✓ **Quick Border**
To create a line border quickly, click the **Line/Border Style** button on the Formatting toolbar and select one of the borders on the **Border** palette.

Adding Special Elements

Need a calendar for the company newsletter? How about a coupon for a customer mailing you're preparing? Maybe you just need a decorative element to draw attention to a headline or make a bland page look lively. You'll find plenty of special elements to add to your publications in Publisher's Design Gallery.

✓ What's In the Design Gallery?

The Design Gallery has numerous objects you can insert and design sets you can use, such as mastheads, logos, reply forms, and more. Use the **Objects by Category** tab to choose specific types of objects to insert. Use the **Objects by Design** tab to insert design sets. You can also create your own objects and save them, then reuse them with the **Your Objects** tab.

Task 28: Using the Design Gallery

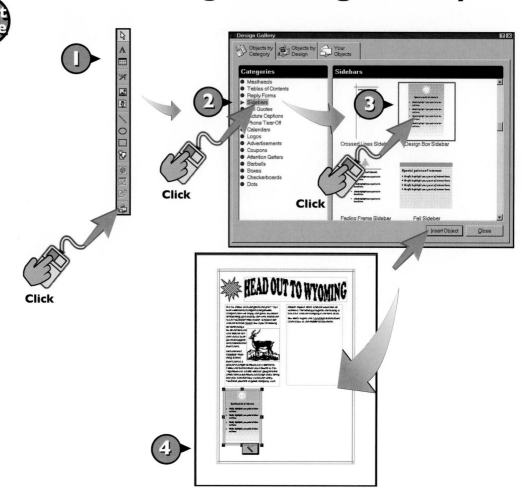

① Click the **Design Gallery Object** button on the Objects toolbar.

② Select a category from the **Categories** list.

③ Select the element style you want to add to your page, then click **Insert Object**.

④ You now can resize and place the object, and make any edits to text just like any other frame.

Task 29: Working on the Background Page

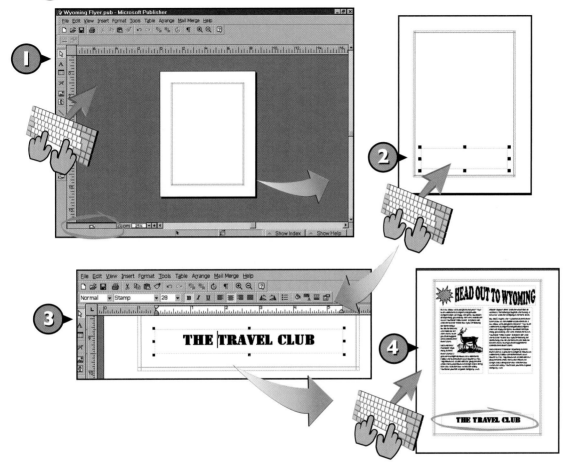

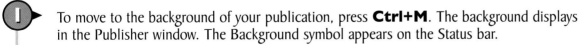

1 To move to the background of your publication, press **Ctrl+M**. The background displays in the Publisher window. The Background symbol appears on the Status bar.

2 Create a text frame and enter the text you want to see on every page of your publication.

3 Apply any formatting to the text using the tools available on the Formatting toolbar.

4 To return to the foreground, press **Ctrl+M**.

Adding Text to a Background Page

Every publication has a background, which sits underneath the pages you create. If you place elements on the background, you can see those elements on every page. The background is an ideal container for page numbers or a corporate logo.

 **Background Tip**
Remember that your foreground pages are usually full of text and graphics. Keep your background text short and near the top or bottom edge of the page, or it won't be seen clearly.

 **Inserting Page Numbers**
Choose **Insert, Page Numbers**. Publisher automatically inserts a page number code in the text box. The code looks like a pound sign on the background; it becomes the page number on the foreground.

Task 30: Adding Background Graphics

Working with Background Graphics

For some of the more professional and polished publications you prepare, perhaps an annual report or some other publication that goes out to the public, consider adding a background graphic that will appear on every page. You can use shapes or graphics you create, clip art, or another scanned image.

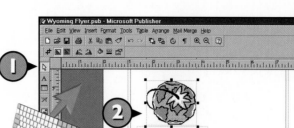

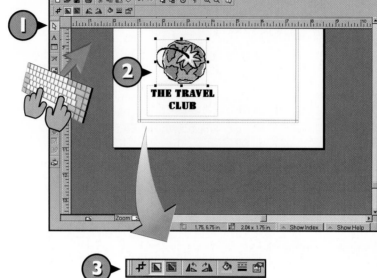

✓ Don't Forget!

To move to the background page first, press **Ctrl+M**. To return to the foreground page, press **Ctrl+M** again.

✓ Background Tip

When you work on the foreground, you must keep graphics away from the location that's directly on top of the background graphic.

1 ▶ Press **Ctrl+M** to view the background page.

2 ▶ Insert the picture frame you want to use, and select the graphic, clip art, or shape to insert into the frame.

3 ▶ Make any formatting changes, such as adding a border or changing shape colors if needed.

4 ▶ Return to the foreground to check everything; press **Ctrl+M** and check your graphic.

Task 31: Making Text Frames Transparent

Using the Transparent Command

It's often effective to place text on top of objects or shapes. However, the text frame you create is, by default, opaque and therefore the frame itself is seen along with the text on top of an object or shape. To avoid this unsightly problem, use Publisher's Transparent command to make the frame invisible as it sits on the object or shape.

Create a text box on top of a shape or other graphic object, then add and format the text you need.

Press **Ctrl+T** to make the frame (but not the text) transparent. The background object shows through the frame.

End Task

Task 32: Using Opaque Text Frames

Working with Opaque Frames

You can create very effective titles and attention getters by placing a text frame on a graphic, particularly shapes. Unlike the previous task, where you learned to make a text frame transparent, another effect is to keep the frame opaque so it covers the object. You can then add formatting to the frame, such as color or a border, to make the frame stand out. Take a look at the example in this task to give you some ideas on using opaque frames in your own publications.

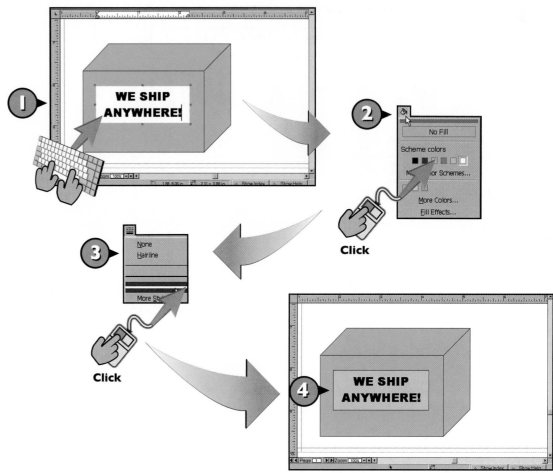

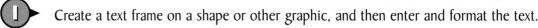

> **1** Create a text frame on a shape or other graphic, and then enter and format the text.

> **2** To add color, click the **Fill Color** button on the Formatting toolbar and select a color or fill pattern (try not to clash with the background graphic).

> **3** To add a border to the frame, click the **Line/Border Style** button and select a border.

> **4** The text frame appears opaque with the formatting changes you set.

Task 33: Creating a Web Page

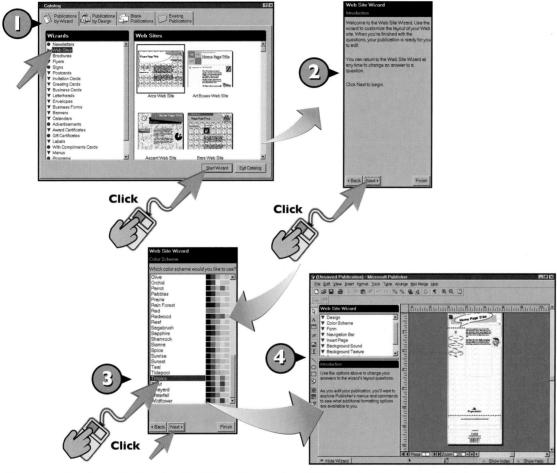

Click

Click

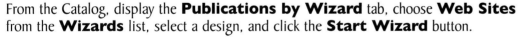

Click

Using the Web Site Wizard

Publisher 98 has a slew of Web designs available so you don't have to create these complicated publications from scratch. You can use the **Publications by Wizard** tab to start a design for an entire Web site, including multiple pages.

1. From the Catalog, display the **Publications by Wizard** tab, choose **Web Sites** from the **Wizards** list, select a design, and click the **Start Wizard** button.

2. The wizard's Introduction appears; click **Next** to begin.

3. Provide information to each wizard question, and choose **Next** to continue, or click **Finish** when you are done.

4. The publication layout is complete.

✓ **Do-It-Yourselfers**
You can also design your own Web page from scratch. Use the **Blank Publications** tab to create a single Web page.

Changing Background Texture

Backgrounds on Web pages are the norm; just check your favorite Web site. After you've designed text and graphics, you might decide that a plain white background is just too dull and lifeless. You can easily change the background by using the **Wizard Background Texture** option.

✓ **Hidden Wizard?**
If the Web Site Wizard isn't visible in the Publisher window, click **Show Wizard** in the bottom-left corner of the screen.

✓ **Choose Another Background**
If you don't like the appearance of the texture you choose in Step 4, click the **Browse** button again and try another texture.

Task 34: Adding a Background to Your Web Page

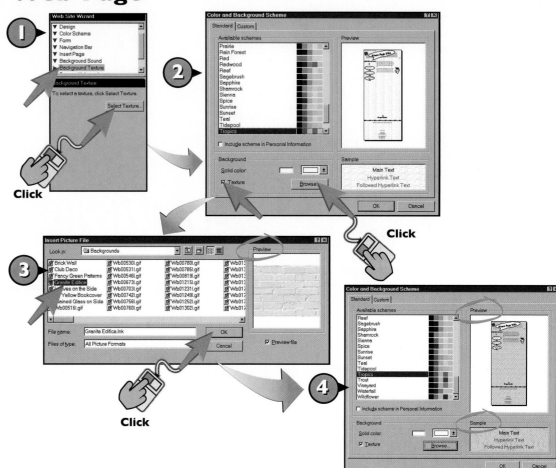

1 ▶ From the Web Site Wizard options, choose **Background Texture**, then click the **Select Texture** button.

2 ▶ When the Color and Background Scheme dialog box displays, select **Texture** and click **Browse** to open the Insert Picture File dialog box.

3 ▶ Click a file to see it in the Preview box. Select the background you want to use and choose **OK**.

4 ▶ The Color and Background Scheme dialog box presents your Web page with the background texture you selected. Click **OK** to apply the texture.

Task 35: Adding a Hyperlink to Your Web Page

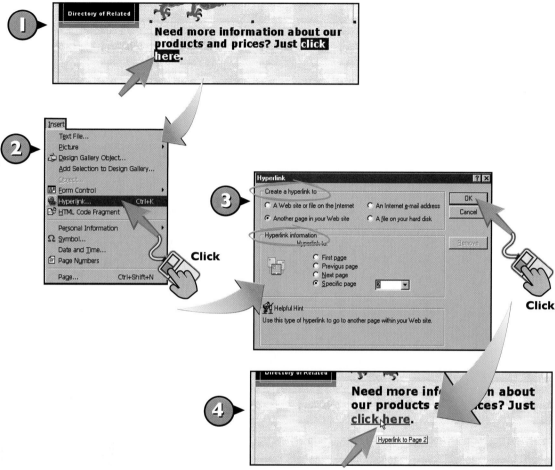

Click

Click

Inserting Links

If you have multiple pages on your Web site, you can insert hyperlinks that give your readers a way to jump from page to page. You can also use hyperlinks to take readers to another site. You can attach a hyperlink to text or graphics (buttons, rectangles, and so on).

1. ▶ Select the object or text you want to use for the hyperlink.

2. ▶ Open the **Insert** menu and choose **Hyperlink** to open the Hyperlink dialog box.

3. ▶ Specify the appropriate location for the link and choose **OK**.

4. ▶ Position your mouse over the object you used for the hyperlink to see a ScreenTip that shows the target.

✓ **Varied Choices**
The choices in the Hyperlink dialog box vary depending on the location of the hyperlink. For example, a Web site needs a URL, while another page on your own Web site only requires a target page location.

End Task

Task 36: Testing Your Web Pages

Previewing Your Page

Don't upload a new Web page publication until you've tested it. The graphics, text, and general layout that looked terrific on your monitor may not translate well to the Web. To check it all out, preview the publication in your browser.

✓ What's Index.html?

When you preview your Web publication, the URL for Page 1 indicates a page named Index.html. That's the usual requirement for Web publications but you must check with your Internet service provider to make sure that's the convention used at your site.

✓ Using Internet Explorer?

Check out Part 5 of this book to learn how to use the Internet Explorer Web browser that comes with the Office Small Business Edition CD-ROM.

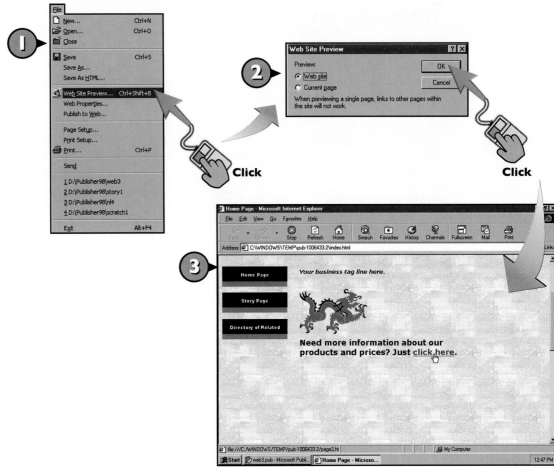

Click   **Click**

1 ▶ Open the **File** menu and select **Web Site Preview**.

2 ▶ Specify whether you want to see all pages (to check your hyperlinks) or just the page you're currently preparing. Choose **OK**.

3 ▶ Your browser opens with your Web publication displayed.

Task 37: Saving Web Pages

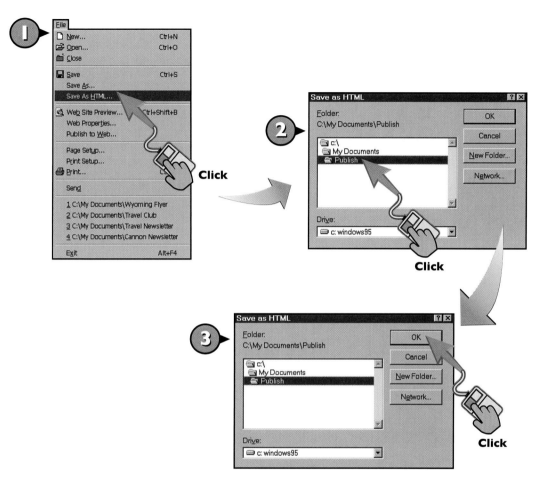

Click

Click

Click

Using the Save As HTML Command

You can save your Web publication to your Web site, a network drive (for an internal site), or to a folder. The reason most people save to a folder is because they're not the company Webmaster and don't have the appropriate permissions to install publications on the real Web site. (Don't forget you have to tell your Webmaster where to find your publication.) In this task, you use the Save As HTML command to save the publication to a folder.

✓ **Publishing Your Page**
To publish to your Web site, you need the Microsoft Web Publishing Wizard. When you installed Publisher, a desktop icon named **Setup for Microsoft Web Publishing Wizard** was installed. Double-click it and follow the instructions.

1 Open the **File** menu and select **Save As HTML**.

2 Choose a folder in which to store the file. (Use the **New Folder** button to create a new folder.)

3 Click **OK**, and the publication is saved as a Web document ready to be published on the Web.

End Task

Internet Explorer

Unless you've been stranded on a tropical island for the past several years, you've heard about the Internet in some form or fashion, and have perhaps already tapped into its power. The Internet, a vast collection of interconnected computers, puts you in touch with millions of other users and oodles of information. The World Wide Web, or Web for short, is the most popular aspect of the Internet these days—an ever-growing collection of documents stored on the Internet that users can access visually using a Web browser program. That's where Internet Explorer comes in.

Internet Explorer is a browser program you can use to view and navigate Web pages. The program comes with Office Small Business Edition (you'll find it in the Small Business ValuPack on the CD). In Part 5, you learn the basics for using Internet Explorer to follow links, download files, perform a Web search, and keep track of your favorite Web sites.

To use Internet Explorer, you need a modem and an Internet connection. Most users sign up with an Internet service provider, a company that's already connected to the Internet and lets you connect via their computers. (If you're connected to a network that's connected to the Internet, a modem isn't necessary and neither is an Internet service provider.)

Tasks

Task 1: Entering an URL

What's an URL?

URL (pronounced "earl") stands for Universal Resource Locator and is an address of a specific site on the Internet. The URLs for Web pages typically use "www" as the first part of the address, followed by the site name (such as "mcp"), followed by the type of site (such as "com" for commercial). Periods, called *dots*, are used to separate each part of the address (www.mcp.com).

✓ What About HTTP?
Some Web browser programs require you to enter the prefix http:// before an URL address. You don't have to do that with Internet Explorer; it automatically enters the prefix for you.

✓ URLs as Links
If you have a document or email message that displays a URL as a hyperlink, double-click it to go to that site.

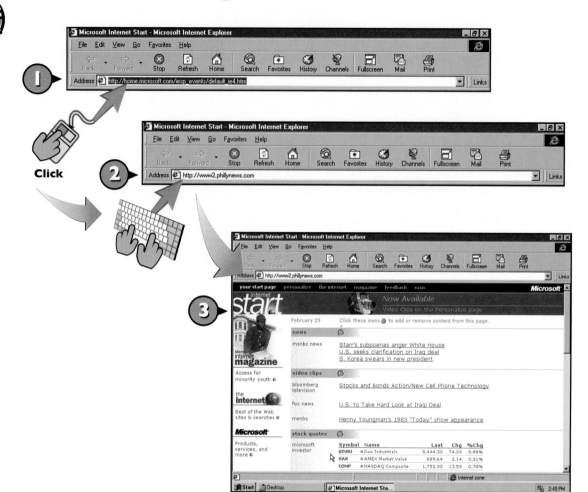

 Click anywhere in the **Address box** to highlight the current listing.

 Enter the URL you want to access. (As soon as you start typing, the existing text is replaced with the new URL.) Press **Enter**.

3 Internet Explorer opens the specified page.

Task 2: Searching the Web

Start Here

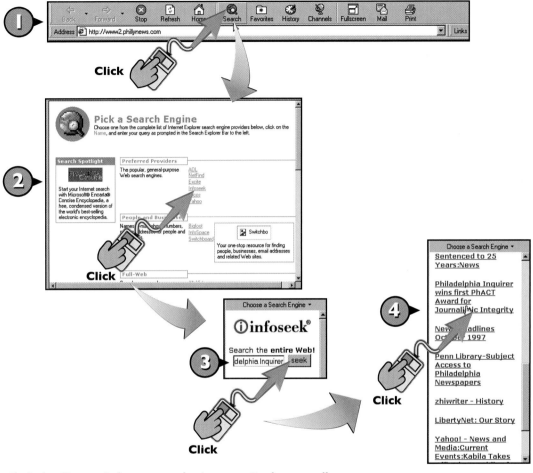

Click

Pick a Search Engine
Choose one from the complete list of Internet Explorer search engine providers below, click on the Name, and enter your query as prompted in the Search Explorer Bar to the left.

Search Spotlight

Start your Internet search with Microsoft® Encarta® Concise Encyclopedia, a free, condensed version of the world's best-selling electronic encyclopedia.

Preferred Providers
The popular, general-purpose Web search engines.

AOL
NetFind
Excite
Infoseek
Lycos
Yahoo

People and Businesses
Names, email, phone numbers, addresses for people and

Bigfoot
InfoSpace
Switchboard

Switchbo
Your one-stop resource for finding people, businesses, email addresses and related Web sites.

Full-Web

Click

ⓘinfoseek®
Choose a Search Engine ▾

Search the **entire Web!**
delphia Inquirer seek

Click

Choose a Search Engine ▾
Sentenced to 25 Years:News

Philadelphia Inquirer wins first PhACT Award for Journalistic Integrity

News Headlines October 1997

Penn Library-Subject Access to Philadelphia Newspapers

zhiwriter - History

LibertyNet: Our Story

Yahoo! – News and Media:Current Events:Kabila Takes

Click

① Click the **Search** button on the Internet Explorer toolbar.

② Click on a search engine.

③ Enter the word(s) you want to search for and click the button to start the search, such as **Seek**.

④ Scroll through the search results. Click the result that seems most promising to move to that site.

Using Search Tools

If you're looking for a particular site or subject on the Web, there are numerous search tools, also called search engines, you can use. Search engines are programs designed to collect and categorize Web sites. Simply type in the word or phrase you're looking for, and the search engine locates any matches. There are dozens of search tools available, and Internet Explorer can help you tap into some of the most popular ones available.

✓ Narrowing Your Search

Many Internet search engines let you enter specific criteria to help narrow your search, such as looking for sites that contain an exact spelling of a word or combination of words. Be sure to check out any tip information available at the search engine's site.

End Task

Task 3: Working with Links

Using Hyperlinks

Another way to move around the Internet is through links, also called *hyperlinks*. Most Web pages you view with Internet Explorer have hyperlinks. They're easy to spot because they display in a different color and they're underlined. When you click on a link, you jump to another Web page.

✓ Locating Links

Not all links appear as underlined text. Some Web pages use graphics and buttons as links. To find out if a graphic is a link, hover your mouse pointer over the object, if the pointer becomes a hand, you've found a link.

✓ Link Colors

If you return to the page containing the original link you followed, you'll notice that the hyperlink has changed color. This reminds you that you've already checked out that particular link.

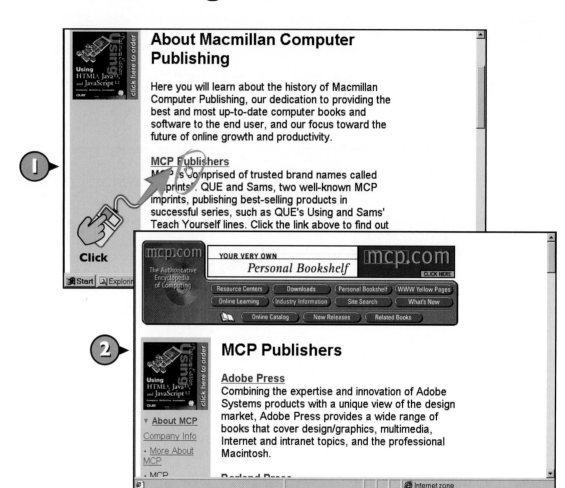

1. Position your pointer over a link. Your pointer turns into a hand icon.

2. Click to move to the Web page for this link.

Task 4: Navigating Web Pages

Click

Click

1 To return to the previous Web page, click the **Back** button. A ToolTip displays information about that page.

2 To move forward through the pages you've seen (after you've moved back), and click the **Forward** button.

Using the Back and Forward Buttons

One of the easiest ways to navigate Web pages is with Internet Explorer's toolbar buttons. The **Back** and **Forward** buttons let you return to Web pages you've previously viewed. For example, you may open a Web page with two links you want to follow. After checking out the first link, you're ready to follow the second. Simply return to the page using the **Back** button.

 Another Navigation Route

To see a list of the URLs you've entered, click the arrow to the right of the Address box. Then select the URL you would like to return to.

Downloading Files

The Internet is a great source of files. Software, information, and even IRS forms can be downloaded. Many files available for downloading include instructions on how to download and install the file. Depending on the size of the file you select, the download may take a few seconds or several hours.

Virus Alert!
The Internet is also a source of viruses, so be sure to run a virus check on any programs you download.

Compressed Files
Most downloaded files are compressed. To unpack a file with an extension .ZIP, you must have the WinZip program. If you don't, download it from http://www.winzip.com. To unpack a file with an extension .EXE, double-click the file in Explorer and follow the instructions.

Task 5: Downloading Files

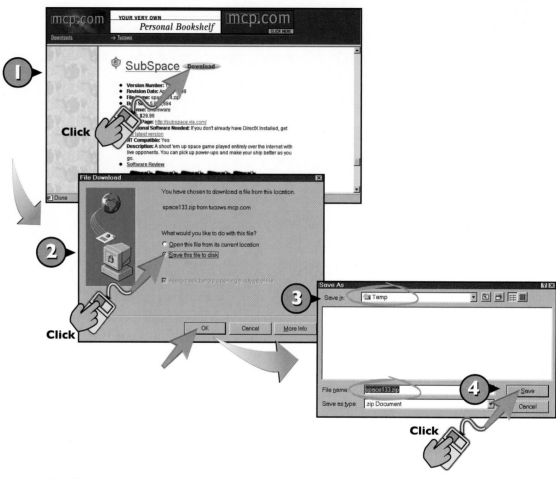

Locate the file you want to download and click its download link.

Select the **Save this file to disk** option and click **OK**.

Select a folder to hold the file, such as a **Temp** folder. (The filename is provided for you.)

Click **Save** and the download begins. When the download is complete, you can access the file on your computer.

Task 6: Printing Web Pages

Start Here

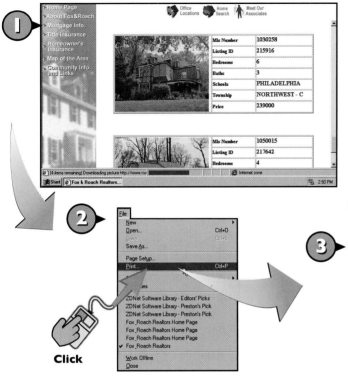

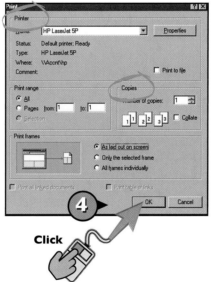

Using the Print Command

When you run across Web pages you want to keep, you can easily print a copy with Internet Explorer's Print command.

Click

Click

Display the Web page you want to print a copy of.

Open Internet Explorer's **File** menu and select **Print**.

Set the printing options you need.

Click **OK** to print the Web page.

✓ **Quick Print**
You can click the **Print** button on the Internet Explorer toolbar to print the page instantly without changing any printer settings.

End Task

Task 7: Saving Web Pages

Saving Pages and Time

If your Internet time is limited, you can save Web pages and view them later while you're offline. Web pages are saved as HTML files. After you save a page, you can open it again in Internet Explorer or another program that lets you view Web pages.

✓ Opening Saved Pages

To open a page later while you're no longer logged on to the Internet, open Internet Explorer's **File** menu and select **Open**. Locate the folder and Web page you saved, then click **Open**.

✓ Copying Web Page Text

If you run across a Web page that has information you would like to copy, you can do so with the **Copy** command. Right-click over the text and select **Copy**. Open the program and file you want to copy to and select **Edit, Paste**.

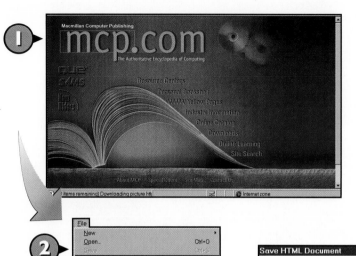

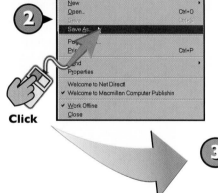

Click

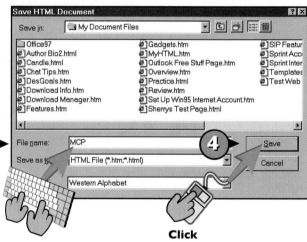

Click

1 Display the Web page you want to save.

2 Open Internet Explorer's **File** menu and select **Save As**.

3 Choose a folder to save the page to and type in a filename.

4 Click **Save**.

Task 8: Personalizing Your Start Page

Start Here

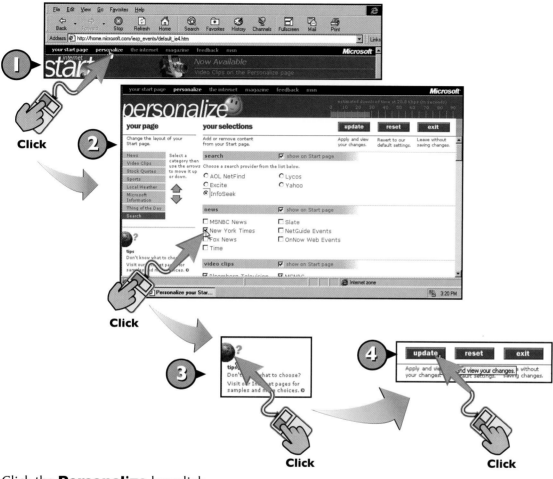

Click

Click

Click

Click

Click

Click

Customizing the Microsoft Start Page

By default, when you first install Internet Explorer, your home page is a page on the Microsoft Web site called Your Start Page. (A home page is the Web page you always start your session from.) The Microsoft start page is filled with links to news, video, stock quotes, and all sorts of other Web features. You can customize which links you want to see on this home page.

1. Click the **Personalize** hyperlink.

2. On the Personalize page, select and deselect the features and options that you want.

3. Click the **Tips** link to visit sample home pages. The site also has additional choices available for your home page.

4. Choose **Update** to save your changes or choose **Exit** to abandon any changes you made.

Change Your Home Page

You're not stuck with the Microsoft start page. You can change your default home page by choosing **View, Internet Options,** and entering a new URL in the **Address box** on the **Navigation tab.**

End Task

Favorite Web Sites

You can automate trips to your favorite Web sites by keeping their URLs in a special list called **Favorites.** This makes it easy to quickly visit these sites again without having to remember or retype their URLs.

✓ Need to Organize?
Turn to Part 5, Task 10 to learn how to organize your favorite Web pages into folders and categories.

✓ Close Favorites
To close the Favorites list pane, click on the **Favorites** button on the toolbar.

✓ Configuration Settings?
Use the **Yes** options in the Add Favorite dialog box to subscribe to the page. This way, Internet Explorer lets you know when the page is updated so you can go check it out, or updates it for you so you can view it later while offline.

Task 9: Adding a Favorite Site

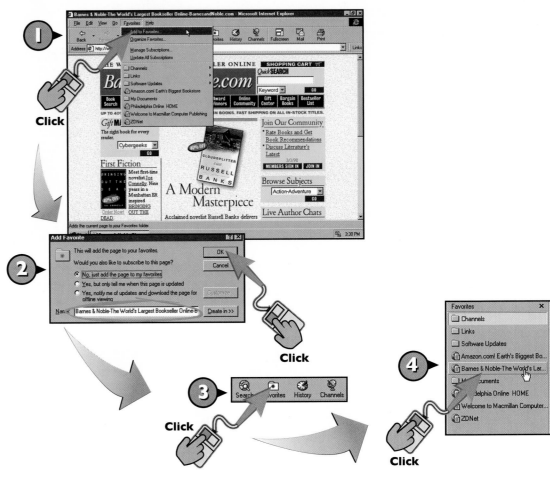

 When you arrive at a site you think you'll want to visit frequently, open the **Favorites** menu and select **Add to Favorites**.

 Confirm the name you want to use for this site. You can edit the name if you want to, then click **OK**.

 The next time you want to access the site, click the **Favorites** button.

 Choose your site from the list to open the page.

End Task

Task 10: Organizing Favorite Sites

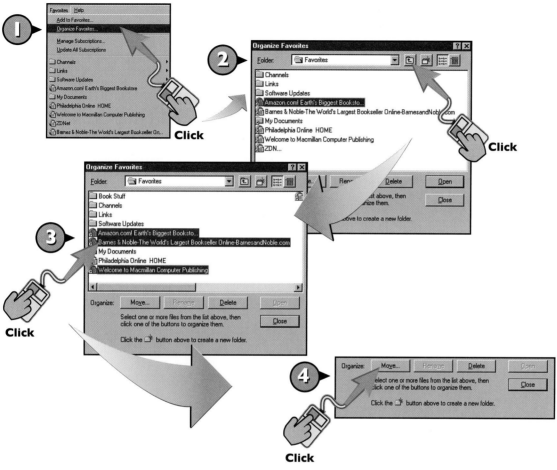

Click

Click

Click

Click

Storing Your Favorites in Folders

After you've been wandering around the Internet for a while, finding exciting and interesting sites, your list of favorites can get out of hand. Some people have lists that are so long they spend more time scrolling through them than it would take to enter the URL from scratch. You can organize your favorite sites into folders to make it easier to find them.

✓ **Already Have Folders?**
Your version of Internet Explorer may come with some premade folders already created for you, but you can easily rearrange, rename, or delete them using the Organize Favorites dialog box.

---

1 Open the **Favorites** menu and select **Organize Favorites**.

2 Click the **Create New Folder** button and type in a folder name to match the category you're creating, such as **Book Stuff**.

3 Select the sites you want to move into the folder. (To select more than one favorite at a time, hold down the **Ctrl** key while clicking each one.)

4 Click the **Move** button; when the list of folder names displays, click the folder you created for this category.

Task 11: Viewing Your Site History

Using the History Folder

Internet Explorer keeps track of every Web page you visit and stores the URLs in a History folder. It saves the URLs for 20 days (the default setting). If you forgot to mark a particular site as a favorite and can't remember where it was, use the History folder to relocate the page.

✓ Changing the History Settings

You can configure the way your History folder works by choosing **View, Internet Options** from the menu bar. In the History section of the General tab, specify the number of items you want to keep in the folder and the number of days to keep the history.

✓ Quick History

To quickly see your current session history, click the arrow on the **Back** button to display a list of URLs you've visited.

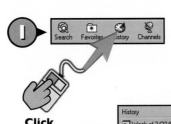

Click

Click

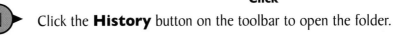

Click

1	Click the **History** button on the toolbar to open the folder.
2	The contents of your History folder display in the left pane. Click the site you want to revisit.
3	To close the pane, click on the **History** button on the toolbar.

End Task

Task 12: Working with Cache Files

Start Here

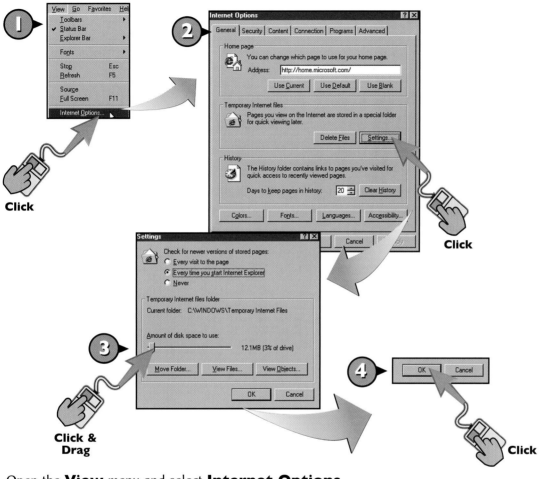

Click

Click

Click & Drag

Click

What's a Cache?

As you move from site to site, Internet Explorer saves the pages in a folder on your hard drive, which is called caching. Each time you move to another site, Explorer checks the folder to see if that page already exists. If it does, it's loaded from the cache folder, which is faster than going out onto the Internet to find the site and load the page.

✓ **Cache Slowing You Down?**
If your computer is running slowly, you can empty the cache folder or decrease the size of the cache to speed things up.

✓ **Clean Your Cache**
Choose **Delete Files** in the Internet Options dialog box to clean out the cache. A confirmation dialog box appears; click **OK**.

① Open the **View** menu and select **Internet Options**.

② On the General tab, click the **Settings** button in the Temporary Internet files section.

③ Use the slider bar to change the percentage of disk space used for these files.

④ Choose **OK** to save the new settings, and click **OK** again to exit the Internet Options dialog box.

End Task

PART 6

Expedia Streets 98

In addition to all the great Office products that make up the Office Small Business Edition suite, you'll also find Expedia Streets 98 as part of the package. Expedia Streets is a map program that enables you to locate addresses and places, plan routes, pinpoint your favorite spots, and more. You'll find plenty of uses for the program that pertain to your small business needs. For example, you can look up and mark the locations of all surrounding competitors, or you can highlight a route to a new client's office and print it out to give to your sales staff. You can even copy the map and insert it into Word documents or email messages you compose in Outlook.

In this part of the book, you learn how to use Expedia Streets 98 to locate any address on the map, measure the distance between two destinations, plan a route for your next trip, and even look up lodging or points of interest along the way and dial into the Internet to make travel reservations. Expedia Streets 98 can help you find your way, whether it's around town or on the road (Expedia Streets 98 is a great tool to include on your laptop computer).

Tasks

Task 1: Finding an Address

Looking Up an Address

Use Expedia Streets 98 to quickly locate addresses around the country. Even if you know only a portion of the address, Expedia Streets 98 can locate addresses that match the criteria you enter and help you narrow your search.

Can't Find It?

Expedia Street's database isn't exhaustive, and some addresses you try to look up can't be found. It all depends on how up-to-date the map information was at the time the database was created.

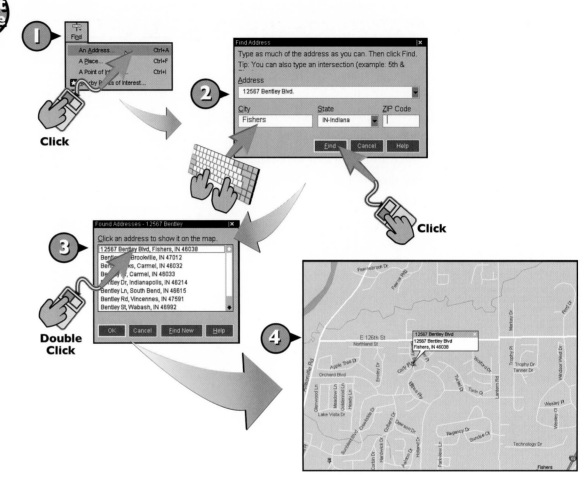

Start Here

Click

Double Click

1. Click the **Find** button on the top toolbar and select **An Address**.

2. Fill in as much of the address as you know in the **Address**, **City**, **State**, and **Zip code** boxes; then click **Find**.

3. When the Found Addresses dialog box opens, double-click the address you want to view on the map.

4. The address is pinpointed on the map.

End Task

Task 2: Marking a Location with a Pushpin

Start Here

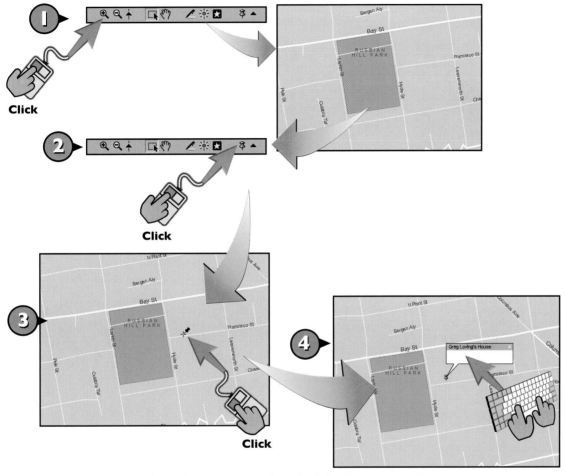

Click

Click

Click

What Are Pushpins?

Just as people do with wall maps, you can place pushpins in your Streets 98 map. This is a great way to mark the locations of customers, branch offices, or even relatives. Pushpins are saved in Streets 98's pushpin folders.

✓ Using Pushpin Explorer

Pushpins are organized into folders, just like other files. For example, any pushpins marked with the Find an Address command are saved in the Found Addresses folder. You can create new folders and organize your pushpins using Pushpin Explorer; open the **Tools** menu and select **Pushpin Explorer**.

✓ Close the Pushpin Note

Click the pushpin note's **Close** button (×) to close the pushpin note balloon.

1 Using the **Zoom** tool from the bottom toolbar, find the location on the map you want to mark.

2 Click the **Pushpin** button on the bottom toolbar.

3 Click on the map location to insert the pushpin.

4 Fill in the name of the location (you can also click inside the note balloon and enter a comment).

End Task

Task 3: Finding Specific Places

Looking Up Places

In addition to looking up specific addresses, you can tap into Expedia Street 98's database to look up places such as cities, parks, airports, and more.

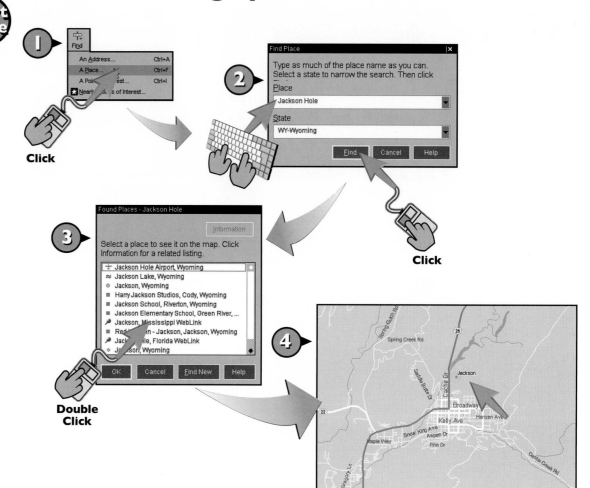

✓ More Information?

To look up information about a particular place listed in the Found Places dialog box, select the place and click the **Information** button.

✓ No Luck?

If the search didn't reveal the place you were looking for, try another search by clicking the **Find New** button in the Found Places dialog box.

1 Click the **Find** button on the top toolbar and select **A Place**.

2 Enter the name of the place you want to find in the **Place** box and the state in the **State** box and click **Find**.

3 In the Found Places dialog box, double-click on the exact location you're seeking.

4 Streets 98 locates the place on the map.

Task 4: Measuring Distances Between Places

Start Here

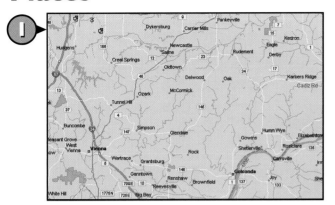

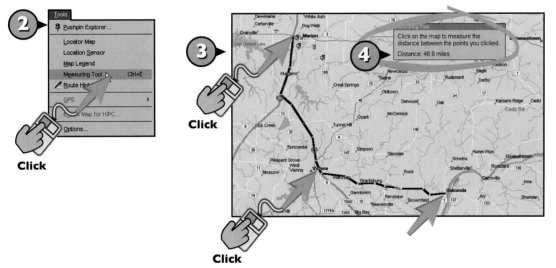

Click

Click

Click

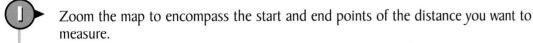

Using the Measuring Tool

Streets 98's Measuring Tool is an electronic ruler you can use to gauge the distance between two points. Use the ruler to measure the miles or kilometers of every bend along the route from point A to point B.

✓ **Want to Measure Kilometers?**
Open the **Tools** menu and select **Options**. Click the **Kilometers** option and then click **OK**.

✓ **Quick Measure**
To quickly measure the distance between two points without including every bend or turn in the road, simply click the **Measuring Tool** once on the start point and once on the end point.

---

1 Zoom the map to encompass the start and end points of the distance you want to measure.

2 Open the **Tools** menu and select **Measuring Tool**.

3 Click on the starting point, then click along each point in the route as needed.

4 A black line traces your route and the Measuring Tool box counts the miles. Press **Esc** to close the Measuring Tool.

End Task

Task 5: Finding Places to Visit

Looking Up Points of Interest

Expedia Streets 98 can help you locate points of interest along any route, such as restaurants, museums, hotels, and more. For example, if you're planning a vacation, look up places along your route you'd like to visit, including addresses and phone numbers.

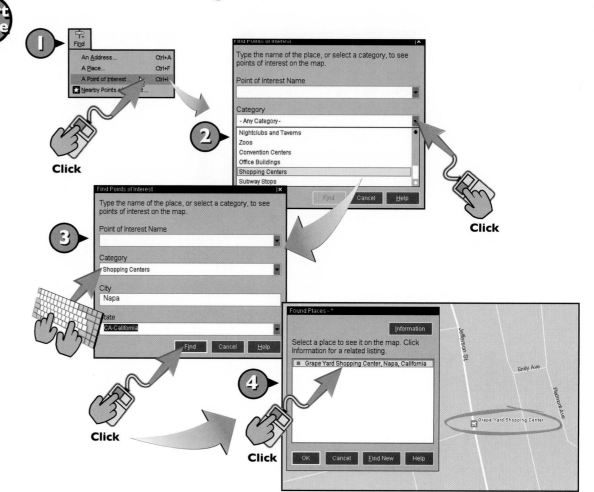

✓ Closing Found Places
To close the Found Places dialog box at any time, click **OK**.

✓ More Info
To find out the address and phone number, click the **Information** button. A Guides dialog box appears with details about the place. Click the **Close** button to close the box.

1 ▶ Click on the **Find** button on the top toolbar and select **A Point of Interest**.

2 ▶ Click the **Category** drop-down arrow and choose the type of place.

3 ▶ Fill in the **City** and **State** text boxes to help narrow your search, then click **Find**.

4 ▶ From the list of found places, click the site you're interested in, and the map shows the location.

Task 6: Choosing a Route

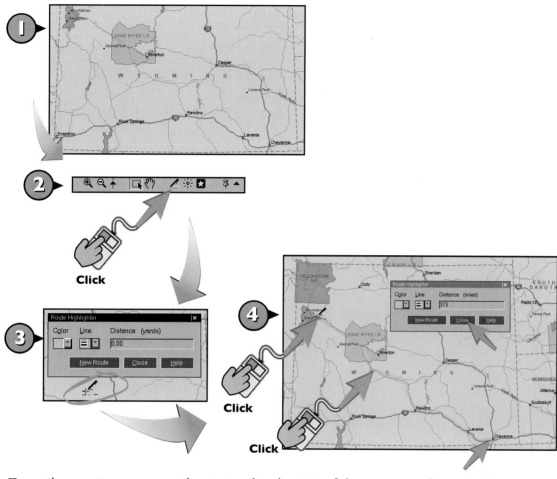

Click

Click

Click

Using the Route Highlighter

The **Route Highlighter tool** lets you draw—right on the map—the route you want to take, and highlights it in the color you specify. You can then print it out to take along with you, or save it for future use.

✓ **Save Your Route**
Open the **File** menu and select **Save Map**. A Save As dialog box opens so you can give the route a name. Next time you want to view the route, choose **File**, **Open Map** and select the route name.

✓ **New Color?**
To change the highlight color used, click the **Color** drop-down arrow in the Route Highlighter box and choose another color. Change the line style with the **Line** drop-down list.

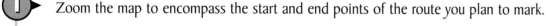

1 ▶ Zoom the map to encompass the start and end points of the route you plan to mark.

2 ▶ Click on the **Route Highlighter** tool on the bottom toolbar.

3 ▶ Your pointer turns into a pen and the Route Highlighter box appears.

4 ▶ Click along the map to indicate the roads you plan to take. Click the **Close** button when finished.

End Task

Task 7: Printing a Map

Printing

You can easily print portions of the map and routes you've highlighted. Simply display the portion of the map you want to print, zooming in or out as needed, then use the **Print** command.

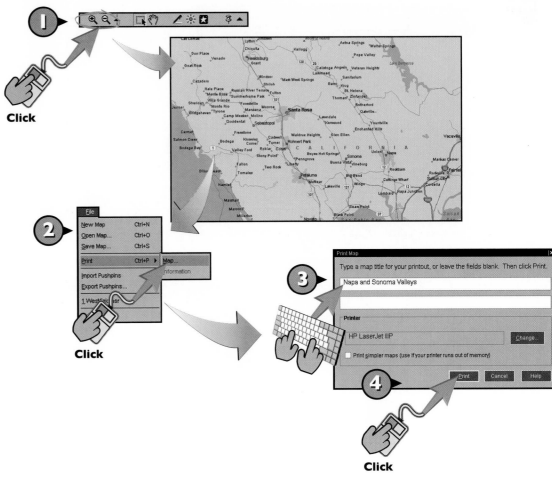

Click

Click

Click

(1) Zoom in or out to the area you want to print.

(2) Open the **File** menu and select **Print**, then select **Map**.

(3) In the Print dialog box, you can opt to enter two lines of title text.

(4) Click **Print** to print the map.

End Task

Task 8: Planning Ahead

Start Here

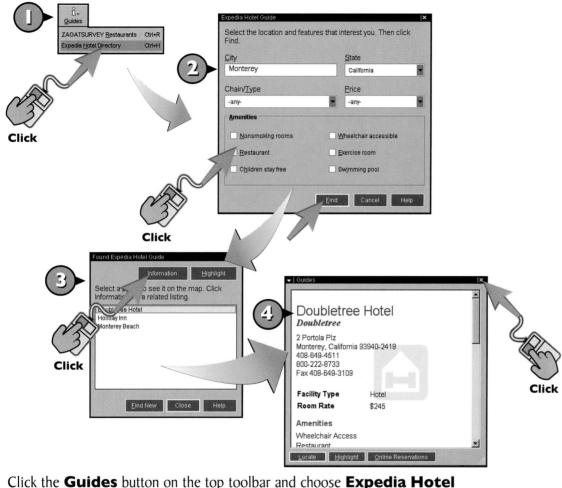

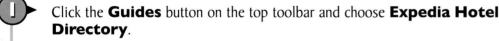

Looking Up Hotels and Motels

You can use Expedia Streets 98 to do even more than provide a map and a list of things to do or places to go. The combination of Streets 98 and the Internet gives you the tools you need to get detailed information about lodging and making reservations.

✓ **Make Reservations**
If there's an **Online Reservations** button in the detailed information box, click it to open your browser and go to the Web site to make a reservation.

✓ **Hungry?**
Use these same steps to look up restaurants anywhere on the map; click the **Guides** button and choose **ZAGATSURVEY Restaurants**.

✓ **Close It**
To close the Found Expedia Hotel Guide dialog box, click the **Close** button.

① Click the **Guides** button on the top toolbar and choose **Expedia Hotel Directory**.

② Fill in information about city, state, chain, or amenities. Click **Find**.

③ Choose a place from the list, then click **Information**.

④ An information page provides details about the hotel. (Click the **Close** button to exit.)

End Task

Small Business Financial Manager

Office SBE comes with a special program designed specifically for small business users—Small Business Financial Manager. It works along with Excel to help you examine, manipulate, and analyze your business data. You can import your accounting data into Small Business Financial Manager to generate reports and what-if scenarios that help you see your financial data more clearly. You can even create charts that help you quickly view how variances in sales, product changes, or expenses affect your data.

Small Business Financial Manager is a collection of useful worksheets and wizards you can use to speculate and forecast how changes in your finances affect your bottom line. As a result, you can make better financial decisions. When installed, Small Business Financial Manager becomes an add-on to the Excel program in the form of a new menu, Accounting, added to the menu bar. You can open Small Business Financial Manager by using the shortcut icon on the Windows desktop or by choosing a menu item on the Accounting menu in the Excel program window.

In this part of the book, you learn how to use several Small Business Financial Manager tools to examine your own business data, including how to import your accounting data into Financial Manager and how to generate different reports.

Tasks

Using the Import Wizard

To analyze your accounting data with the Small Business Financial Manager, you must first convert it to a format that the Small Business Financial Manager can use. You can do this by using the Small Business Financial Manager Import Wizard. With Excel open, select the **Accounting** menu and choose **Import Wizard**.

✓ **The Prompt Box**
A prompt box appears warning you it may take a while to import your data. Click **Yes** to continue (unless you have a large amount of accounting information, it should only take a few minutes).

! **Importing Large Files**
If you're importing extremely large accounting files, you won't be able to use your computer for any other tasks during the import process. You might want to perform the import at a time when you won't be needing your computer.

Task 1: Importing Accounting Data into the Small Business Financial Manager

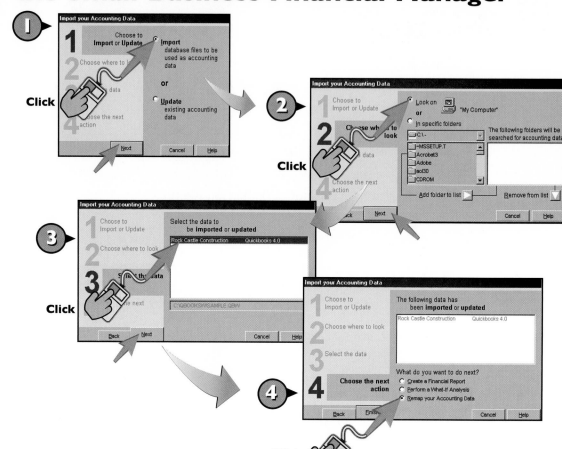

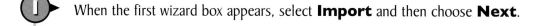

① When the first wizard box appears, select **Import** and then choose **Next**.

② Choose **Look on "My Computer"** and click **Next**. The wizard searches your computer for your accounting files.

③ Highlight the accounting data to import and choose **Next**.

④ Select **Remap your Accounting Data** and click **Finish**. Move any misplaced categories to the proper locations.

Task 2: Creating Financial Reports

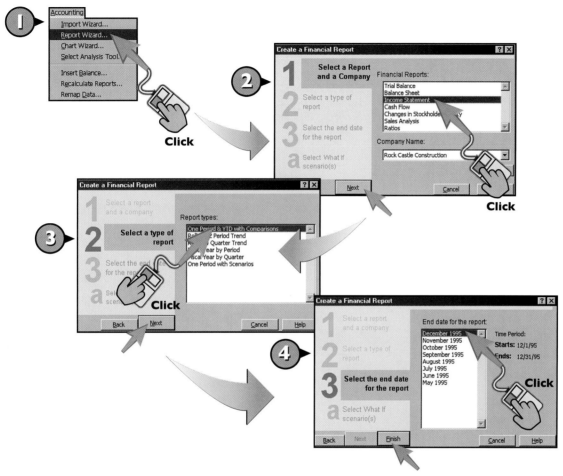

Click

Click

Click

Click

Using the Report Wizard

After you've imported your accounting information, you'll want to begin using it to create financial reports. The Report Wizard enables you to create a variety of reports that can paint a clear picture of your financial health.

✓ Using the Startup Screen
If you start the Small Business Financial Manager from the desktop icon, you can click **Report** on the opening screen to start the Report Wizard.

ⓘ Your Steps May Differ!
Keep in mind when creating your report that the steps you encounter may vary from those presented here, depending on the report you choose.

✓ Click Help
For a description of each report, click the **Help** button in the wizard dialog box.

---

1 With Excel open, select the **Accounting** menu and choose **Report Wizard**.

2 Highlight the report you want to create, select a company from **Company Name** drop-down list, and choose **Next**.

3 Choose a report type from the **Report types** list and click **Next**.

4 Select an end date for the report and choose **Finish**.

Task 3: Saving a Report

Saving a Report

Very often you'll want to keep a report for review at a later time, or to show to your accountant or financial advisor. You may even want to include it in a presentation that you're putting together. Whatever the reason, you'll need to save it to disk to access the information again without having to re-create the report.

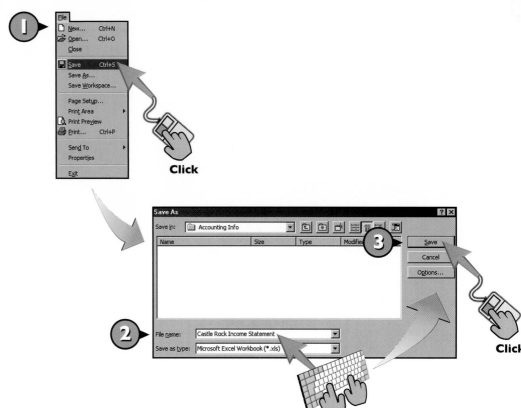

Click

Click

✓ **Quick Save**

For quick saving as you continue to work on the report (after you've saved the first time to give the file a name), just click the **Save** button on the toolbar.

✓ **File Formats**

Any reports you create using Small Business Financial Manager are saved as Excel files with the **.XLS** file extension.

① After you've generated a report, open the **File** menu and select **Save**.

② The Save As dialog box opens so you can choose a folder in which to save the report and assign a filename.

③ Choose **Save**.

End Task

Start Here

Task 4: Printing a Small Business Financial Manager Report

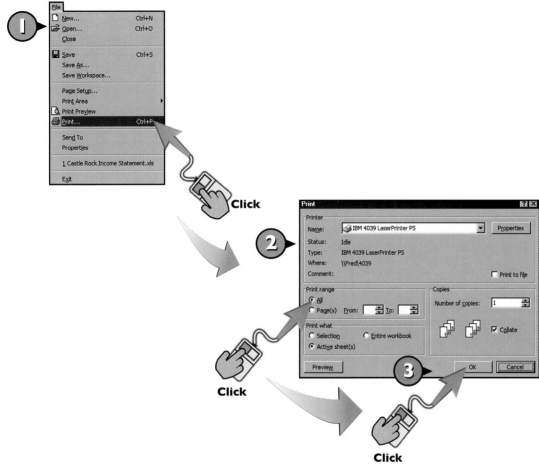

Click

Click

Click

Using the Print Dialog Box

Unless you plan to gather everyone in the office around your desk to see the reports you create on your monitor, you're going to want to print a hardcopy of your reports. Use the Print dialog box options to change printers, print several copies, and more.

✓ Quick Print
If you don't need to make any changes to the printer options before printing, click the **Print** button on the Standard toolbar to start printing the report immediately.

✓ Need Help?
See Part 2, Task 24 to learn more about printing with Excel.

1. Begin by opening the report you want to print and choose **File**, **Print** from the menu bar.

2. Set any necessary options before printing, such as which printer to use or how many copies to print.

3. Choose **OK** to print your report.

End Task

PART

Task 5: Creating a Balance Sheet Chart

Using the Chart Wizard

When it comes to understanding complex financial data, there's nothing like a picture to bring it all together. While reports and analyses let you scrutinize the details, charts let you grasp the bigger picture visually in a split second. Use the Chart Wizard to whip up professional charts based on your accounting data.

✓ Your Steps May Differ
Remember that the steps you encounter may vary depending on which chart you decide to create.

✓ Need Help?
For a description of each chart available, click the **Help** button in the first wizard dialog box.

✓ Copy and Paste
You can include a chart in a **Small Business Financial Manager** report by copying the chart and pasting it into the desired report.

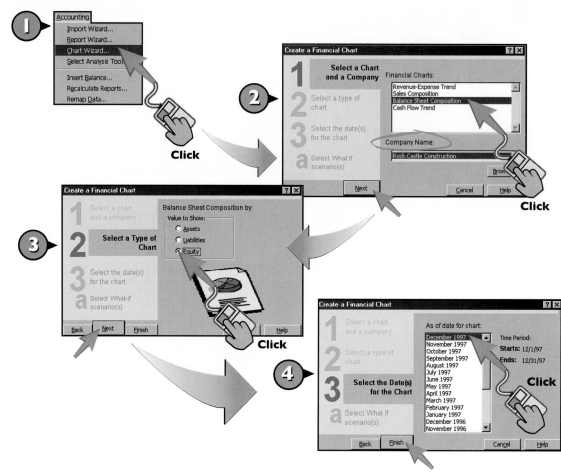

Open the **Accounting** menu and choose **Chart Wizard**.

Select the chart you want to create, select the company to use for the chart, then click **Next**.

Choose the balance sheet component you want to use as the basis for the chart and click **Next**.

Select an end date for the chart, then click **Finish** to create the chart.

End Task

Task 6: Creating a Business Comparison Report

Start Here

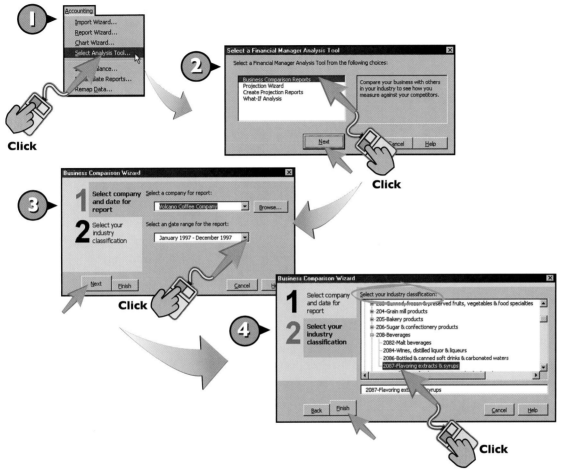

① Click

② Click

③ Click

④ Click

Using the Select Analysis Tool

One new feature included with the Small Business Financial Manager 98 is an analysis tool that lets you compare your financial data against the averages for companies in your related industry. The data for the Business Comparison Report is provided by Robert Morris Associates.

✅ Other Analysis Tools

You can also create a Projection Report and perform What-If Analysis scenarios with the other Analysis Tools available. Your steps will vary slightly from those described in this task, but the procedures are very similar.

✅ Need to Make Changes?

You can change the company, date range, or industry classification by clicking the **Change Wizard Choices** hyperlink on the report.

① Open the **Accounting** menu and choose **Select Analysis Tool**.

② Choose **Business Comparison Reports** and then click **Next**.

③ Select the company to use and the date range for the report. Click **Next**.

④ Select the industry classification that most closely matches your business. Click **Finish**.

End Task

active document   The document that is currently selected in your software window.

alignment   The way text lines up against the margins of a page.

AutoText   Text that is corrected automatically. You can invent a string of characters that will autocorrect itself to a word or phrase.

background page   In Publisher, a virtual page that holds elements you want to repeat on every page of your publication.

cell   An area in a worksheet or table that holds a specific, individual, piece of information.

cell data   Any information, including number, text, and formulas, that is contained in a worksheet cell.

chart   A graphic representation of a selection of workbook cell data.

clip gallery   A collection of clip art, pictures, sound files, and video clips that can be used to spruce up Office documents.

Design Gallery   In Publisher, a gallery of predesigned and preformatted special elements you can add to a publication.

dialog box   Any of the information boxes that appear during the installation or use of an application and require input from the user.

docked toolbar   Any toolbar that is attached to one of the four sides of an application window.

Document Map   A vertical display of the headings in a Word document. Click on an entry to move quickly to that part of the document.

drop-down list   A list of choices presented when you press the arrow to the right of a field in a dialog box.

fields   Placeholders for data that changes, such as a date, a mail-merge field, or a page number.

floating toolbar   A toolbar that is not anchored to the edge of the window, but instead displays in the document window for easy access.

gutter   The space on a page left blank for binding. (The left edge of a right page, the right edge of a left page.)

hard copy   Computer jargon for a printed copy of a document file.

highlight   Add a band of color to text by using the Highlight tool on the Word toolbar.

justification   Aligning text so that it fills the area between the left and right margins.

layout guides   In Publisher, guidelines you put on the background page, representing boundaries for all pages in your publication. You can also use these guidelines to align objects.

macro   A method of automating common tasks you perform in certain applications such as Word or Excel. Users can record keystrokes and mouse clicks so they can be played back automatically.

Office Assistant   Animated Office help system that provides interactive help, tips, and other online assistance.

paste-up   In Publisher, a method of laying out individual parts of a document to prepare for professional printing. For instance, you may print the text and paste photos.

path   The name of the folder (or multiple folders) needed to locate a file, separated by the backslash character. For example: My Documents\Letters\Mom.Doc.

PIM   Personal Information Manager software (such as the Contacts folder in Outlook), in which you track information about contacts as well as keep notes on your interaction with those contacts.

placeholder text   Text that is inserted automatically in a field or a Publisher text frame. It is replaced by your own text.

Replace   A command on the Edit menu that you can use to replace text with different text automatically. This feature can also be used with codes such as tabs and paragraph marks.

ruler guides   In Publisher, guidelines representing ruler positions that you place on a page in order to line up objects. Also called Ruler Marks.

scratch area   The portion of the Publisher window outside the page display. Use the scratch area to "park" frames you want to move to another page.

ScreenTips   Notes that display on your screen to explain a function or feature.

shortcut keys   Keyboard combinations that provide shortcuts for menu commands. For example, Ctrl+S is a shortcut key for File, Save.

Shortcut menu   The menu that appears when you right-click on an object.

Snap To   In Publisher, a feature that forces objects to a specific position on a page.

TaskPad   In Outlook, a list of tasks that displays when you use the Calendar folder.

template   Available in Word, Excel, and Publisher, templates provide predesigned patterns on which Office documents can be based.

Text Overflow icon   In Publisher, a button at the bottom of a text frame that indicates whether the text in the frame is continued in another, connected text frame.

watermark   A pale element placed in the background of a document page. Used for graphics or special text such as "Confidential."

workbook   An Excel document that contains one or more worksheets, chart sheets, or VBA modules.

worksheet   In Excel, the workbook component that contains cell data, formulas, and charts.

Outlook 98

What's New in Outlook 98

At first glance, several things about the new Outlook 98 jump out at you. The newest involves Internet Explorer 4.0. Internet Explorer 4.0 comes with Outlook 98 and automatically installs when you install Outlook. If you already have Internet Explorer 4.0 installed, you don't need to install it again. The bottom line here is that Outlook 98 absolutely will not run without Internet Explorer 4.0 installed.

After you have Outlook 98 installed, you notice a number of obvious changes right away. For example, the Office Assistant is now available in Outlook as well as in the other Office components. The next obvious change is that the default opening folder is now Outlook Today rather than the Inbox.

Outlook Today is not a folder but a page (everything from Microsoft is increasingly being molded to emulate the Internet). Outlook Today gives you a quick, current look at your Outlook 98 information. You see the number of unread messages in your Inbox, as well as any appointments or tasks scheduled for today.

The next change to the basic Outlook interface is the reorganization of the Outlook bar. Outlook now has only two default shortcut groups, Outlook Shortcuts and My

Shortcuts. The Mail and Other shortcut groups have been replaced by the My Shortcuts group. Depending on whether you're doing a fresh Outlook 98 install or installing over Outlook 97, you'll find a different configuration of shortcuts.

Not so obvious—but very handy—is the capability to customize Outlook 98 toolbars. By double-clicking a blank spot on either the Standard or Advanced toolbar, you can open the Customize dialog box and use it to add and remove commands from the menu bar and the toolbars and change their appearance. You can even create your own custom toolbar.

Using Outlook 98 Email Features

As mentioned earlier, the Mail shortcuts group is no longer available on the Outlook bar; therefore, you may want to add shortcuts for the Outbox and Sent Items folders if you use them frequently.

The real changes to email in Outlook 98 are substantial and behind the scenes:

- Services have been replaced by Internet Accounts.

- Faxing is now available in Outlook.

- The new Address Book automatically culls the Contacts folder for entries. You must import an existing Exchange Personal Address Book into the Address Book to use it.

- Remote mail has been eliminated.

- You can now choose to send only or to send and receive email during an online session.

- The Rules Wizard and support for multiple Internet service providers are now part of Outlook 98, no longer requiring an enhancement patch.

- Junk and adult email filters have been added to Outlook 98, enabling you to sort out undesirable email before it hits your inbox.

Other Changes to Outlook 98

As you use the menus and toolbars, you'll note a number of changes, including moved, modified, or new commands. For the most part, the basics are all intact, with some additions and improvements.

Getting Organized

One handy new item that appears on the Standard toolbar in every folder is the Organize command. Clicking the **Organize** button or opening the **Tools** menu and selecting **Organize** opens the Organize area (also referred to as a *page*).

The Organize page varies from folder to folder. The most common way it enables you to organize your information is by folders, views, or categories. The Inbox Organize page offers by far the most extensive set of organizing tools.

New and Improved Find

The Find feature has been updated to fit Outlook 98's new "Webified" attitude. When you click the **Find** button on the Standard toolbar or open the **Tools** menu and select **Find**, a Find page appears above the Information Viewer.

The Advanced Find feature is the old Outlook 97 Find feature with a few enhancements.

In addition to the more conspicuous modifications in Outlook 98, numerous changes have been made to forms and dialog boxes—some practical, some cosmetic. All in all, you'll find many improvements.

F

G

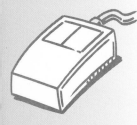